Time Cap

by Nick Rucker

DORRANCE
PUBLISHING CO
EST. 1920
PITTSBURGH, PENNSYLVANIA 15238

Dorrance Publishing Co
585 Alpha Drive
Suite 103
Pittsburgh, PA 15238
Visit our website at *www.dorrancebookstore.com*

ISBN: 978-1-6470-2493-2
eISBN: 978-1-6470-2717-9

NICK AND I FIRST MET IN IRAQ IN 2010 when we were in the 1st Maintenance Company under the 541st Combat Sustainment Support Battalion. It was a quick passing in the makeshift gym at Camp Liberty, Iraq, and maybe a handful of words were spoken between us. Initially, I thought he was your typical specialist who just wanted to do his work and go back to the hooch to watch movies and play Xbox, but I soon learned he was not your average Joe on deployment. After that deployment, we both ended up in the same company in 1ID, 4IBCT heading to Afghanistan, and after I retired and Nick separated, he lived with my wife and me for a while. Since that first encounter in the Camp Liberty gym, I have witnessed a transformation within him, and I've seen firsthand the toll two deployments have taken on him and his personal life; I have also seen how he has turned that around and made the decision to be a better person and make his own successes.

What's great about this book is it is compiled from real-time excerpts over the course of his two deployments and the methods he used to deal with all of that when he returned. It gives a personal account of his thoughts and fears and all the same worries that most soldiers face while deployed. They aren't the worries of possible death while conducting combat operations or adrenaline-filled stories of kicking in doors and shooting people in the face, only to deal with the consequences later; they're real thoughts that most average "regular

Joes" have while making the long walk to the DFAC or while lifting weights to pass the time. This book is a look at what most soldiers think when they have time to reflect on the decisions that have led to where they are at the time, and I believe is relatable to anyone who has ever deployed.

Perhaps the most favorable takeaway I got from this book is to know how well Nick overcame the diversity, the bad decisions and the self-destructive behavior that came with his battles with alcohol and depression. I have seen for myself his transformation from that naïve young SPC on his first deployment into a hardened veteran of two wars on the outside and countless wars within. There's no doubt anyone who reads this will find something in it to relate to. Some may find inspiration and motivation; some may read it and reflect on their own deployments and life afterward. Whatever you take away from this book, I hope reading it makes as positive of an impact on you as knowing Nick has made on me.

Erik Sprague, CW2, Retired, U.S. Army

12 Oct. 08

"That piece of shit deserved everything he got!" said my dad, a veteran of Desert Storm. He said this to me the first time I brought up Saddam Hussein around him after Hussein's death in 2006. When I was a kid, I remember my dad telling me stories of the Highway of Death in Kuwait that led to Iraq. American, Canadian, British and French aircraft destroyed the retreating Iraqi army as they fled Kuwait in 1991. I had heard it from his mouth when I was a kid, and now, I am here in basic training learning about it from a PowerPoint presentation and some videos. I wanted to raise my hand and tell everyone in the room that my dad had been there and seen it first hand, but I didn't. It wasn't worth drawing extra attention to myself, not here during basic training.

I kept his boot camp graduation picture with me in a Ziploc bag for many years. The photo sat inside a cardboard display case that also had a calendar attached to it and said "U.S. Army" on the top. The edge of the photo of my dad had been chewed on by a mouse at some point, but it was my dad, and I was proud to have the photo. In that same Ziploc bag, I had photos of my dad in Saudi Arabia. Some of him with camels and with his buddy while he served during Desert Storm. I was five when he shipped off to war. I spent most of that time collecting Desert Storm trading cards that Pro Set put out of different military vehicles and commanders who were in charge, like Norman Schwarzkopf and President Bush.

The big thing at the time was the yellow ribbons that folks would display that signified "Bring our troops home." I had decorated my bicycle at the time with two of those ribbons and wore my chocolate chip Desert Storm shirt and boonie hat that my dad had sent me to a parade in our hometown on the 4th of July. My dad is the main reason I joined the military. I grew up in the small town of Hopkins, Missouri, and really didn't experience much of the military while growing up besides the pictures and stories my dad told me. He and my mom divorced when I was two, and I didn't see him much, but I always remembered the stories he told me when I did see him. He had a hard time talking about the war, and I was too little to understand why it was difficult for him. He never has shared much of those stories. I suppose one day he will want to share them, and I'll gladly listen. When I decided to join the Army myself, he was on the fence about it. His first reaction was, "No kid of mine is going to join the Army. I did enough time for all of us."

I had recruited out of St. Joseph, Missouri, and my recruiter, Sergeant West, couldn't have made the process any easier. He was a great guy. I had always heard horror stories of guys joining the military and getting screwed over in some way, but Sergeant West really had his recruits' best interests in mind. He hooked me up with a good job, and upon completion of basic training and MOS school, I would be a 91G or fire control systems repairer. I would be fixing military optics and working on tanks. It sounded cool at the time, and he said it would be a lot better than being a cav. scout, which was the other job I was offered. I really had no idea what to expect from any job the Army offered, but he said if you go 91G, you can get a $20,000 sign on bonus, and that's where he got me. I went through MEPS in Kansas City, and after walking around in my underwear for some old man who was the doctor at the in-processing station, I had passed the physical and was well on my way to starting my life in the Army.

As I sat signing my life away on those papers during final processing in Kansas City, the guy I was talking to told me I would be going to Fort Knox, Kentucky. *I thought, Wow, this is perfect because that's where my dad went to basic training, I'm just following in the old man's footsteps.* I got home that day and felt like a new man. The day I left for basic training, my mom drove me to Maryville where I met Sergeant West at the Break Time gas station just outside of town. That was the first time that the reality of what I was about to do hit me. I started to get a little homesick, especially when my mom and sister were crying in the parking lot as I loaded up my stuff. I knew I wouldn't see them for at least three or four months, and I think that's the longest I had gone without being around my family. I got in the van to go to the airport; I swallowed the lump in my throat and said goodbye. I still remember that even now, two months down the road. I feel like I finally grew up that day and was ready to face the world on my own.

Bootcamp at Fort Knox, Kentucky. What can I say? It's been interesting. I miss a lot of things back home. I left Hopkins in August, and this has been the first time that I've been able to write any personal notes or even keep a journal. Music is the main thing that I miss the most. I do wish I had someone to write letters home to besides family. I look at the photos in other guys' lockers here, and it seems like they've all got a girl back at home waiting on them. I bet that's a good feeling. I don't, of course, and that's all right for now. I will meet someone someday. I keep thinking that I'll meet an Army girl at AIT, or maybe once I get to my first duty station. Who knows what will happen?

Life is way different in the Army. It's very strict, and it took a little time to get adjusted, but I am enjoying it. There are some guys here that keep it pretty interesting. I met my buddy Hanks while we were going through in-processing. He is from somewhere in Washington, and we share a lot of the same interests in music. We roomed together while we were going through in-processing. He was going through training to become a cav. Scout, so we are in different companies here. I've only seen him once since we started bootcamp. He was in the chow hall walking out as I was standing in line getting ready to eat. In the chow hall, you have to stand in single file, and you cannot look around. You literally have to stare at the back of the head of the guy in front of you or run the risk of getting punished by the drill sergeants. I saw Hanks that day as I was standing in line. I looked over at him and kind of gave a thumbs up with my hand down by my side at the position of attention. As soon as I did that, I heard Drill Sergeant Yanetsko yell, "Fucking Rucker, go to the end of the line, you piece of shit!" It was worth it, but I haven't seen Hanks since.

Private Scott is one of the guys who keeps it interesting for us. He once locked himself in the cleaning closet, and in order to get out he had to scream, "HELP ME," at the top of his lungs before the drill sergeants would get the key and let him out. He did this for about 30 minutes before they finally gave in. I'm no expert on guys who probably shouldn't be in the Army, but Private Scott was one of them. He eventually got kicked out a while back. He honestly couldn't keep up with the rest of us, and he just wasn't doing so great in classroom work, so they sent him home.

There are a couple guys here that are in their forties. One of them was going down the tower on the confidence course. Somehow his boot got caught the very top of the tower. All you heard was him scream on the way down. Luckily he landed right on the mats that are under the tower, or he would've for sure snapped his neck. From what I heard, the drill sergeants told him after that, "Man, you're an old dude, and we totally understand if you want to throw in the towel and go home," because honestly I think anyone that experienced that fall would probably want to go home. Last I knew, he packed his stuff up and hit the road.

Rivera is another one who has been on the drill sergeant's radar for a couple of weeks now. One morning, we all were awoken at 3:00 A.M. to the sound of Drill Sergeant Cruz screaming from the laundry room. We had no idea what he had done this time, but it was obvious by the tone of his voice that it wasn't good. He walked out into the hallway and told us all to stand by our bunks. He walked by us one at a time holding a cell phone. We aren't allowed cell phones, so we knew that we were all in deep shit.

Drill Sergeant Cruz said, "I just found this in the laundry room tucked behind the dryer. Now I will give you until the count of five before we are all outside doing burpees until you're dead." No one made a sound. We were outside doing burpees and crawling through a sandbox for hours after that. Still, no one came forward and said a thing.

We all went back inside after our smoke session and tried to figure out whose phone it was. Unfortunately, no one was coming forward. Later that day, we were all standing outside in a circle when Drill Sergeant Schlink came out holding the phone. He walked around looking us all in the eyes. At that point, we all felt guilty and like it was our cell phone. He walked slowly around and then stopped and said, "You assholes know whose phone this is and guess what, after a little research and a phone call to Sprint I know whose phone it is too." The suspense was killing us. Then he screamed, "RIVERA!"

We all knew he was screwed. Rivera started crying and throwing a fit. He was in the national guard in Puerto Rico, and none of us could understand anything that was coming out of his mouth, but obviously he was crying, and the rest of us were pissed because he had us crawling in the sandbox at 3:00 A. M. in the morning. To say the least it has been interesting here. They didn't kick him out, though. I think the paperwork for that is too much work for the drill sergeants.

I've been a squad leader for a while now with Tierney, Shaw, and Snyder. I'm learning a lot about myself. Learning what I am comfortable doing and what I'm not comfortable doing. One of the most uncomfortable things I've done so far is rappel down a 70-foot tower. That took a lot of balls to do at the time. I knew there was no way out of doing it, so I just convinced myself that I wouldn't die, and just did it. So, I've just been trying to do all those things that make me uncomfortable, so I can get better.

We went to church on Sundays for a while. It was nice to have that hour to ourselves, and some of us took turns looking out for one another, so we could get some extra sleep. They finally caught on to us and told us if anyone was caught sleeping while at church, there would be hell to pay. None of us went to church after that because of how boring it was in the first place. Sundays are for cleaning if you don't go to church. So, we pull all of our stuff out of our lockers and clean everything. We pull our beds away from the walls and clean under them. We sometimes push our beds together and hide out under the furthest bunk away closest to the wall, so we can sneak in a nap when we get the chance.

I'm still ready to get out of here and on to Aberdeen Proving Ground. I've been here two months as of tomorrow. It doesn't seem like it's been that long at all. What's strange is how long I've been around the 60 of these other guys, and I feel like I barely know them. Boot camp feels like a transition period – a melting pot of personalities that are all here for the same purpose, which is just to get through boot camp and move on with our lives. We just have to make do with the people we have around us and hope that we all get through it together. To make a machine work, you have to figure out within yourself where exactly you fit in. Every man here has to figure that out for himself. As time has moved on, the machine starts working better and in unison. There are those few who just never really find their place in the machine, and they end up going home. As for Rivera, I imagine that is probably where he will find himself eventually.

Tomorrow is our second physical training test. That is two minutes of pushups, sit ups, and a timed two mile run. I passed the first one when we got here, which was a relief. I've never really been one who has practiced pushups, sit ups, or running, so I feel like passing that was quite an accomplishment. All of the running we do now has me feeling pretty confident that I'll do well. I suppose we will find out soon enough just how far I've come. I'm in pretty decent shape now. We eat pretty clean food, and we don't have any sugar. I can't remember the last time I actually had sugar. My body just feels better all around; I don't feel like a huge pile of shit at least. I think when I get home, people will notice a big difference. I look in the mirror now, and it's like I barely even recognize myself. I think this is the skinniest I've been since birth.

13 Oct. 08

I passed that PT test this morning. I ran my two miles in 14 minutes and 30 seconds on the dot. As I was passing the finish line, Drill Sergeant Cruz hollered, "Rucker, what did you eat!"

I felt good about it and knew that it would be easier this time around because of all that training that we've done. We've been granted a phone call today, and I'm thinking about calling my dad. I want to talk to him because it feels like it's been forever. We will probably only get about five minutes to talk, but that will be just enough time to tell him I'm doing well and in good spirits. I miss my dad the most of all. I think it's probably because he'd been here at Fort Knox when he went through basic training in the 80s. I want to see if he remembers any of the stuff that I am experiencing. I'm sure he will.

Passing that PT test also means that I secured my graduation spot. As long as I don't fuck up between now and then, I'll be fine. After the PT test, we went on a 15K road march to a fake FOB out in the middle of nowhere where we are spending the night. We basically learned patrol formations on the way here and how to move together as a unit, so when we go on patrol at some point in our careers, we know what we're doing. The best part right now is sleeping out at this FOB. It means that we have one week left of boot camp. I still feel like I haven't learned a damn thing. I feel like the training goes so fast that you get just a few hours to pick up on a new skill before you're off to learn the next one. It's not enough time to really grasp any of the concepts.

I'm interested in reading back over this in a few months when I know where I'll be stationed. A part of me wants to go overseas, then another part wants to stay here in the States. I remember when the wars first started in Iraq and Afghanistan. I was just about to graduate from high school, and I watched on TV soldiers walking the streets of Baghdad and thought I could never do something like that. At the time, I don't think I would've even made it through basic training. Well, here I am now, about to finish basic training, and I still feel as though I may not have the courage to walk the streets of Baghdad. The thought of deploying is a little overwhelming. I keep thinking I'll be just one of the guys that stays here in the States during his whole time while in the Army. I probably shouldn't worry about that now though; I've got some time before that will happen.

26 Oct. 08

I don't get to write as much as I want. I'm afraid that the drill sergeants will find these writings and will put them on display for everyone to see. I think it's important to journal and keep these memories because one day I will get to read back through this and remember all these times that really suck right now but probably won't seem so bad in 20 years. I still wish I could write every day, but unfortunately, it's just not possible. I hopefully will be able to remember most of boot camp. It's been a good experience so far.

Today has been cold. I got punched in the face at breakfast. The kid barely connected with my face though. I was attempting to solve a dispute between two other guys, and then I just found myself in the middle of the argument. There was a little pushing and shoving, and then I got whacked right in the face. I didn't even get angry. I feel as though right now we are all stressed out and are acting on our emotions. Had I gotten angry, and it turned into a fight, that would probably be the deciding factor on whether we both graduate or not. Nothing was said of the altercation, and we just went our separate ways. I honestly don't even know what the argument was over. It was probably something ridiculous that had to do with who got more food than the other.

We have gotten more freedom since we got out here to the FOB. This morning I actually got in a 20-minute nap, which has never happened since we started bootcamp. I haven't heard music in for almost two months now. I remember a while back we were on a bus headed somewhere for training and George Strait's "I Saw God Today" came on the radio, and it felt like I hadn't heard music in years. Immediately, my entire mood just changed. I perked up a bit, and I felt like I was back home. I've loved George Strait since I was a kid. When the movie and album came out, I watched that movie a million times, and I listened to that album so much that I knew every word from front to back. Hearing King George was like meeting an old friend – a little piece of home to get me through this last part of boot camp. Music is pretty powerful, and in that moment, I felt pretty powerful. Once the drill sergeants heard it, they turned it off, but I'd heard enough to lift my spirits.

When I get back home, things are going to be a lot different. My friends and family will see that I have changed, and my new perspective is sure to change how I see them as well. Over the past few months, I have made friendships through collective hard work, earned the respect of my drill sergeants and fellow soldiers, and faced a lot of my fears. Failure was my biggest fear. I doubt anyone who knew me well believed I would be able to make it through basic training and become a soldier. Hell, I wasn't sure myself. But I gambled on myself, and I won. I think the pain of returning home if I failed boot-camp outweighed any pain I have felt while I've been here. I often thought to myself if I failed and got sent home what would I do. I don't think I would return home, I would probably move to some random state in the United States and never return to my hometown again. I would feel that much shame. I'm just glad it's not going to come to that.

Since we've been out here, it's been pretty cold. I think you spend enough time out in the cold and your skin kind of gets a leathery feeling to it. At least right now that's how I feel. Things have been stressful out here on the FOB, and we've only been out here a day. We don't get a lot of sleep as it is, and pulling overnight fire watch leaves some of us with even less. I think everyone is ready to be done with basic training and move on.

On our way out here, we climbed the big hills of Fort Knox. My dad told me about the hills before I left. They're called Misery, Heartbreak, and Agony. They were no joke either. Those hills are extremely steep, and with an extra 60 pounds on your back, they really test you. We did a 12-mile ruck march out here, and I think that's probably why we are all stressed. We are out of our element and things are tense. Everyone is short tempered with each other, and it's difficult for us to work together on tasks because we keep snapping at each other. We had been staying in the barracks for so long that I think a lot of these guys are stressed out because now we're out here in these tents where it's cold and miserable. They're pushing us to the max of our capabilities, and honestly, some of the guys are struggling because of it.

My mom sent me some photos a while back of my family. When I am feeling down, I pull those out and look at them. She also sent me a Dallas Cowboys football schedule, and I have been keeping up with the scores of the games when I hear them. So many times during boot camp I've found myself just having to find a special place in my mind where I can go to momentarily escape this place. Almost like a Zen feeling of just complete relaxation. I think it's necessary to have those moments. If I don't have those photos with me that my mom sent, then I just think about them, and it makes me feel better.

I remember one of my first journals entire I ever wrote. I was 10 years old, sitting in front of the TV watching a movie about wolverines, and I had just received a copy of *Nintendo* magazine. I remember watching that show and sitting on the carpet in front of the TV and how the carpet was really comfortable and how I could've fallen asleep right there watching that show about wolverines. While I am here, I think back to times like those, and it helps pass the time. If I feel like things are getting tough, then I remind myself that life would be a lot worse if I got sent home. The few times I have gotten to call home have been pretty brief. I spoke with my grandparents once. I knew they would be the main ones that would want to hear from me. They let me know that everything was going well on the farm in Iowa and that they were sure excited to come see me graduate. That was another reason I didn't have trouble finding reasons to keep going. I wanted to make them proud and have them drive here to Fort Knox and see me graduate. I feel like I haven't accomplished much to be proud of up until this point in my life, and now graduating from boot camp will be a really good thing for me.

I love thinking back to times on the farm at my grandparents' house. I would spend summers picking up square bales of hay with my grandpa. It would be blistering hot outside, and he would be on the tractor, and I would be walking behind the trailer throwing bales up. I spent one week cutting thistles for him. This was the first time that he trusted me with a job by myself. He gave me the keys to his pickup and a machete and showed me where the thistles were. I spent three solid days in that field cutting thistles by hand and loading them in the back of the truck. Late on the third day, my legs and arms were all cut up, and I was exhausted, but I was finally done. Grandpa told me after I got back to the house to get in the truck because we were going to go look at my work. As soon as we pulled up to the pasture, we looked up on the sun setting on the hill. You could barely make them out, but there were five thistles still standing on the hill.

He didn't even have to say a word. I just hopped out of the truck and grabbed my shovel and made my way to the hill. I had spent so much time alone out there in that pasture I forgot what ground I had actually covered, and it all started to look the same. I made him happy though once it was all said and done, and he wrote me a check for $100. Looking back now I wish I hadn't taken that money and just let him keep it. At the age of 16, you really need to be learning the lesson of hard work rather than working to get paid. I think one day I'll just write Grandpa a check for $100 and tell him thank you for teaching me all the lessons he has over the years.

31 Oct. 08

It's been a rough few days, but we finally made it. It's around 0130, and it's been quite a night. We left the FOB and started our 12-mile ruck march back. The first three miles weren't too bad. I've had a knot in my back the size of a silver dollar most of boot camp, and I think it's mainly from carrying my weapon at port arms over the past eight weeks. During the 12-mile ruck march back, we stopped to do our nick at night training. We went single file into a concrete trench. We all got lined up; I stuck my head above the trench to see exactly what we were getting ourselves into. All I could see was barb wire spread out about 12 inches above a giant sand pit. I tried to see just how far the sand pit went, but it was so dark I couldn't see the other side.

I looked at my buddies in the trench. We were all exhausted, and you could see in everyone's face that we just wanted to get this last hurdle done. I stuck my head up one more time and was able to make out what looked like one of those bunkers that was on the beach of Normandy during the D-Day invasion. The hole in the front of the bunker was lit up red, and I could see what looked like a 240B. That's when the drill sergeant saw me sticking my head out and told me to keep my fucking head down. I got back down in the hole, some gun fire sounds started to echo, and it sounded like people screaming and across the speaker system. We heard what sounded like yelling in a foreign language. It was obviously something that was recorded and meant to make the experience more real, if that was the case then it was working. We were all starting to get impatient and wanted to get this course over with.

I watched *Jarhead* shortly before I left for boot camp. There is a part where they shoot rounds above these guys' heads while they low crawl under barb wire and have explosions going off all around them. As soon as I started putting the pieces together, the drill sergeant said, "All right guys, keep your heads low and get across that field as fast as you can."

Holy shit, we were about to get shot at. I had once experienced getting shot at while deer hunting when I was a kid. It was a mistake and had just been by chance that two of us were hunting in the same area at the same time, and there had been a ricochet. This was different though.

The drill sergeant said, "Get ready! GO!"

As soon as we got over the wall, gunfire broke out above our heads. My helmet got caught initially on the barb wire, but I think that adrenaline itself is what helped me get it undone from the barb wire. I have never crawled so fast in my life. Those rounds weren't close, but they were close enough to make you fucking crawl fast. As we made our way across, there were explosions going off, and I think since it's Halloween, they had pumpkins exploding as well. At least I felt like it was pumpkin that was hitting me in the helmet as I crawled. I was the first one across the field and basically did a nose dive at the end into the trench on the opposite side. We all made it safe and sound and then geared back up with our rucksacks and started our nine miles back.

This last ruck march was a killer. The first three miles weren't bad leading up to nick at night, but the rest was a struggle. I was in the front with the other squad leaders and went back to check on the guys in my squad. One of them, Solomon, had been marching, and his rucksack had started to fall apart. When I got up to him, I noticed half of his rucksack was dragging on the ground behind him. We were about to reach Heartbreak Hill, and before I could even say anything, one of the other guys grabbed the broken part of his rucksack and tied the strap in a knot against the frame, and it made do for the rest of the ruck march.

I was out in the front with my buddy Tierney. We didn't talk much, but I think we both knew that we had to lead the way. I'm really glad I've spent boot camp with Tierney. He's from Brooklyn, New York, and I think the first person that I've ever met from New York. We just both had the same mindset during our time here. We knew what had to be done to graduate, and we both made sure that we did it.

It is great to be back at the barracks. Even though my back is just destroyed at the moment, the ruck march and training were worth the pain. We graduate soon, and I'll get to see my family, most of whom are planning to come. I feel like I finally have achieved something that is bigger than me. I can finally hold my head up high and be proud in front of my family. It has been a long time since I have felt like I've been able to do that. The pride I will see in all their faces is worth all the pain and homesickness I have experienced here.

Baghdad
Diaries

1

I HAVE SPENT YEARS OF MY LIFE DEDICATED TO SELF-DESTRUCTION. Not until the day I reach Kuwait do I finally feel as if I'm not fighting a never-ending battle with myself. What I want to do and what I am capable of doing finally synchronize, and I can focus enough to take charge and lead myself into battle. Finally, I am able to push forward and make progress beyond the futility I had felt for so many years. To feel the heat, to feel the sand hit my face and push through my pores making my skin feel like rawhide – it is what I want. This frames an identity within me, and there is no more complaining; there are no more excuses. Everything that I have ever imagined and ever wanted, I know I will find in Iraq.

I spend two weeks in Kuwait going through hours of training and hours of waiting... And waiting. The fear and excitement I feel are like nothing I have ever felt before. We board a C-130 bound for Baghdad, Iraq. At 0200 hours, we start loading bags and preparing to leave. Finally, at 1100 hours, our plane is leaving. I take my spot along the wall of the plane. A C-130 has rows of seats in the middle and net seating along the walls. From the uncomfortable look on everyone's face in the middle, I know I probably have the best spot on the plane. Everyone is worn out from being up all night. The sergeants and the specialists who have been here before seem relaxed and are joking around and at ease. Among those of us who have never been here before, though, I can feel the tension. I can see in some faces the fear of where we are about to land. For me, it is a tossup between the two. I am excited, and yes, I am afraid of what is to come. I grew up hearing my dad's stories of war during his time overseas, but I know it will be different for me. This is my life, and this is my story.

We land in Baghdad. The heat is killing us all as we unload the bags. At this point, I am looking forward to not seeing half of these people the rest of the year I am in Iraq. It isn't that they are bad people, but their attitude when under stress and in the heat makes me want to keep away from them as much as possible.

There's nothing "soldier" about being here. The feeling that you'll see action or that you will feel unsafe at all just isn't that common anymore. I guess some people would call us lucky, but as for me and my friend Machen, we are disappointed. From the time we got here till now, we still talk more and more about going 11B infantry with the guys who are actually fighting the war and not just supporting it. I won't be satisfied until I either feed my fear or scare the living hell out of my senses. The thought of not staring death in the face leaves me feeling somewhat belittled at times. If I am going to be looked down upon by my superiors and told what to do by my chain of command, I want to be in a position where I feel like I am making a difference and not just on the sidelines waiting to go home. Sergeant Major Williams will change all that.

We get to our rooms and settle in. We have formation after formation. I think they are trying to find everyone and make sure everyone is still alive. With so many of us, having that many formations makes a lot of sense. One guy hides out for two weeks before we actually know he's here, so accountability is crucial. The last formation I go to, First Sergeant Trunck asks for a volunteer to work for the

Sergeant Major doing construction and for anyone with construction experience to come forward. There are two of us. I haven't done any construction in my life, but something tells me to go for this – that I will force myself to learn a new trade. The guy who is up here with me says, "You can do it man. I don't really want to." His backing out is good because I will be the only person interviewing for the job, but it is also bad because I have no idea what I'm doing. My interview is tomorrow, and I am nervous as hell because I know I'll have to bullshit about my experience in carpentry.

2

I END UP BEING NERVOUS FOR NO REASON. I explain that I know how to use power tools, and I'm pretty good at figuring things out. At the end of the interview, Sergeant Major Williams slides a coin across the desk and says, "You're now a member of the 260th CSSB."

The rapport I am building with Sergeant Major Williams is great. He's something of a father figure to me, and I want his approval, so I work hard to make him proud. I had given him my word that he wouldn't regret choosing me for this job, so I don't want to let him down. I also don't want to get too full of myself in the process.

I honestly believe that during the first two months of this deployment, I have grown so much. I feel my confidence level rising because I am keeping myself mentally in check. My self-awareness keeps me pretty level headed, so it's hard not to say, "Yes, I would stay here longer if I had to." Not for a second have I ever longed to be back home.

I wonder if one day someone will look back and ask me if I was ever a part of the war in Iraq. I don't think I'll know how to answer that. My respect for others in past wars doesn't seem to reflect what my overall assumption of what war truly is. This is the end of a war, not the beginning. As fragile as this situation is, I believe that eventually this will once again become the beginning of a war. Then it will become everything I have envisioned. Maybe not this time, but once again we will have our presence known in the Middle East.

My heroes have changed over the years. They are no longer idols placed upon a pedestal. They are faceless strangers I've never met who quietly appear in the darkness. Their experiences differ from mine, but the emptiness is the same – the emptiness that is there when nothing exists at all. A thousand screams down a dark hallway, inviting anyone in, yet never getting a response is war in its purest form. Then one day you finally hear a second screaming voice, and you never knew it was coming.

1 Oct. 2009

The mortar attack to top all mortar attacks. I am sitting in my room on my computer watching television. At the same time, I hear the impact of one mortar and then another and another. I walk towards the door and put my hand on the handle. I close my eyes and picture a fireball shooting through the door at me as soon as I open it. I slowly fall into the fetal position and think of home – not the home that was my everyday life, but the home that I know is a comfortable home with my friends and family. But they are 7,000 miles away. I open the door just in time to hear, "Incoming! Incoming! Incoming!" As I step out onto my wood porch, I look at the T wall in front of me with rebar sticking out of it. At that moment, I hear the whiz of a rocket shoot overhead and then the mini gun go off. I feel that it is time to go, but I just stand there unable to move – unable to connect my mind with my body. I picture all of those photos they showed us of soldiers blown up in Iraq, the blood, the yellow fat, the burnt skin, and know that I am next and hope I won't have to survive the pain of living through that. I have cried a lot tonight. For the first time since being in Iraq, I wish I were home.

Some days you feel like you could live here the rest of your life with the sand beating on your face and making you a part of this desert. Then other days you feel like you'll never see home again. It's Christmas, and I see people complaining that they can't get out to be with their family because they're snowed in. I guess I feel like even just being in the United States would be enough for me. I remember coming home from San Diego after I had been discharged from the Marine Corps. I made it all the way to Kansas City and slept on a bench with everyone else who was snowed in. I just wanted to be home so badly. I felt like I was in the worst of situations, having to jump another bus to get to St. Joseph only to find out I might get stuck there. My aunt and uncle came to St. Joseph and picked me up, and I felt like I had escaped from death that day. But that wasn't the worst situation I could have been in. I realize that now.

3

I DON'T LIKE TO SAY OUR SURROUNDINGS SHAPE WHO WE ARE TODAY because how we see ourselves is who we truly are. Our circumstances don't define us. How you see yourself is how you really are. Internally, things are always changing, but it may take time for others to see a physical manifestation. My going from sleeping on couches to being here in Iraq may not seem like a beneficial life change to others, but it's exactly where I want to be. I am living my dream, a dream my father helped shape. My love of my current situation stems from the stories he told me when I was a kid. Stories of his military service in Saudi Arabia and the first Iraq war. This is where I need to be, and I feel that with every ounce of my being.

I lived in Maryland at Aberdeen Proving Ground for seven months for AIT. It seemed like it would go on forever. At about the midway point, we were allowed to go about and do what we wanted to on the weekends. There was one guy, SFC Schaefer, who was a total asshole. He was a stickler for rules and regulations, and he loved singling out the ones he thought weren't toeing the line. We all bitched and complained about him all the time. My three friends and I were sitting around at a bar in Baltimore that weekend bullshitting – just getting drunk is what it came down to – when a couple guys sat down by us. My friend McCray, whom we all called Cookie, started talking to them, but I didn't pay much attention to what they were talking about.

Cookie looked over and said, "Hey, Rucker, that guy is a master sergeant at Aberdeen."

I started talking to him a little while just about what to expect once we got out into the world of active duty army. Then I started complaining about SFC Schaefer. As soon as I started talking, I heard my inner voice say, why are you complaining about something you're only going to laugh about in the future? I still finished the sentence. I believe I said, "I hate the sergeant we have in our platoon." That was it.

At that point the inevitable came around and bit me right in the ass. The master sergeant said, "Why do you hate him?"

When you complain you have to defend those complaints, and I had no response. I had willingly walked into a lion's den that I had constructed myself. That lion was me. I have analyzed that situation over and over in my head many times because it's a good reminder to me to keep my mouth shut. Needless to say, I learned my lesson. The sergeant wasn't really the problem at all. The problem was that I chose to complain rather than to affect any kind of change. There would never have been any reason to complain if I had challenged SFC Schaefer beforehand and stood up for what change I really wanted to see.

Eventually, towards the end of AIT, I did challenge him. I challenged him on something that I apparently knew more about than he did. When I did say, "I believe you're wrong here, Sergeant," he didn't handle it well. He decided that extra duty was a way of correcting my questioning of who was right and who was wrong. I drew the short end of the stick, of course. My class of seven people were right beside me when all of this took place. I was to have extra duty that night after class was over. My classmates had told me that day that they were going to go to extra duty with me because they felt that he was wrong also in what he had done. When we got to the orderly room, all eight of us were there. We went up to him and I said, "Sergeant, I'm here to report for extra duty."

He said, "What are these other people doing here with you?"

Then Byrne said, "Sergeant, we're here because we believe that if you're going to punish Rucker for something that we all believed to be right, then you need to punish all of us." I don't think he knew what to say.

I said, "I apologize, Sergeant, for questioning your authority like I did, but I felt that I was right in doing so given the situation."

He said, "Well, Soldier, you don't have to worry about extra duty. I think it's great that you guys came together up here, and I wish we could see more of that. That's why I'm rough on you guys. I want you all to be better." It was too easy to figure out now that it was one incident that has stuck with me for the long haul.

4

MY FAITH IN MYSELF GIVES ME STRENGTH, and my identity is grounded in that strength. My back could be killing me on a 12-mile ruck march, but the pain doesn't matter because I am at the front with my buddies. In the gym for countless hours, pushing my muscles to their absolute limit never seems meaningless because doing so helps me gain Sergeant Villa's respect. He saw something in me that I had not been aware of myself. Under his tutelage, I've become an instructor for close quarters battle. Because he has faith in me, I have more faith in myself. Sgt Villa has not only taught me more about physical toughness but mental toughness as well.

Prior to joining the army, I always wanted to wear the uniform and wear the black beret. Tonight, in the gym, all I can think about is wearing the tan beret of the Army Rangers or the green beret of the Special Forces. Sergeant Villa won't allow me to be complacent. I had achieved one goal, and he made me believe more was possible, whereas in the past I would have been satisfied with what I had already accomplished. I am left asking myself, where did this person come from? My inner voice has always challenged me not to accept less than the best, but my idea of what is best is starting to change. I am beginning to have loftier goals. Sergeant Villa has raised the bar.

I can't stand to hear anyone I work with complaining because I know we have fellow soldiers currently in Iraq, like my friend Hanks, who can't talk to his family like we can every day, who doesn't know where he is sleeping from day to day like we do, and he never complains. He loves every minute of it. His attitude motivates me to work harder and to give to those here who work just as hard right along beside me. My NCO Sergeant Egli is one of those people. I've learned a lot from him in the six months that I've been here. It seems that in everything I do, I am always lucky to find someone who busts his ass more than I do, and Sergeant Egli is that person. He is a model NCO, and I've learned a lot from him. In the military, you pick up different leadership qualities from a lot of different people. You hear about what you're doing wrong more often than you hear about what you're doing right. There are very few atta boys, but at the end of the day, you always know you have someone watching your back, no matter how the day ended.

That kind of love is something that you wouldn't be able to find in a whole lot of places. That's why it's hard to ever imagine leaving it behind. It's even harder at times to read some people's posts on social media bashing the military and praising the Al Qaida for being the weaker force and rising up against us. I suppose everyone is entitled to an opinion, and there are always those who believe in anarchy and overthrowing the government, but they wouldn't last a minute in Afghanistan or Iraq amongst the terrorists that they praise. Like the church group just down the road from Fort Riley and that woman who pickets at soldiers' funerals. I've gone online and read these damn posts about picketing at a soldier's funeral, and nothing gives me more chills or more anger than thinking about it. Freedom of speech is great, but at what point is the line drawn that says shut the fuck up or you're getting your ass kicked? I think that we would all gladly make room on a military flight to bring their asses over here, drop them off at the front gate and say, "You want to bitch and complain about what we do here, you can stand right outside the gate and do it. Good luck!"

I've read this book a couple of times. I read it once while I lived in Kansas City in a one-room studio apartment with another guy from Hopkins. We each slept and lived in the same room. He had his futon on one wall; I had mine on the other. There was no privacy whatsoever, but that year and some change that I lived in that room and read book after book on mastering your life, I slowly came to realize that I was hitting a quarter-life crisis. I knew I was in a dark place, but I didn't realize how far down the rabbit hole I had fallen until I read. My roommate had a thousand books, it seemed. They lined the walls of our apartment. They were stacked in the bathroom. We used them to hold up shelving. We tore out the previous pages to use as bookmarks for following points in the books we were reading. I always found myself asking my roommate for literature on war and people overcoming great odds. I picked up the book not knowing what it was about at all. I chose this book because I was fighting a battle within myself and trying to figure out what to do with my life.

I started reading this book, and it was about a man during the peak of the Vietnam War being drafted and the days leading up to his leaving for basic training. He ran away and spent time at a lodge where he planned to spend a couple days before crossing the Canadian border to avoid the draft. The book wasn't like one I'd read before. It's is based around pre-deployment to Vietnam and stories through his deployment, but he tells the story in such an elegant fashion that it can really be incorporated into any situation in your life. One part of the book has always resonated within me so much that the morning that we were leaving to come to Iraq, I had sudden anxiety attack. I pulled the book out and flipped through the pages. Finally, I found what I was looking for – the story of the last day before he could either leave for Canada or return home and follow through with the draft.

He was paddling out on a lake, and he couldn't see the border into Canada, but he said that he could feel the border like it was right there. He said, "But it was like a dream," he wanted to reach for it, and he held his hand out, but in his dream, something kept him from fully extending his arm. He began to cry because he felt the integrity check hit deep in his gut. It wasn't like anything he had ever gone through. That's when he decided that he wanted to live for the experience. He put aside all of the thought of what you could accomplish in the army and competition and decided that he would live for the experience and that is all. He said in the end that this was what he felt kept him alive through the entire time he was in Vietnam. I put the book down that morning and felt a great sigh of relief.

That book has always been one that I've kept close. It also marked my outlook on being here in Iraq, because when I look at a tube of toothpaste, I don't think that this is just another tube of toothpaste. I think, I bought this tube of toothpaste at the Maryville Walmart and brought it with me 7,000 miles across the world. This tube of toothpaste will one day be trash here in Iraq, but for the time being it is a connection to home. It's easy to get caught up in the politics of war, and people sometimes forget that it's more important just to live for the experience. This outlook has helped me quite a bit. I think that everyone should read this book if they get a chance.

5

I'VE BEEN HERE FOR SIX MONTHS, and I'm already a different person. I remember the tension I felt on the plane coming over here, the fear I had, and the enormity of death. I don't feel those things anymore. The camaraderie that I feel with my fellow soldiers gives me a sense of belonging. This is my home, and these people have become my family. Spending six or seven months together in the harshest conditions has drawn us close. That makes it even harder when those new family members of mine leave to go back to the United States, and I am stuck here.

We have to figure out a way to stay sane, and we do it through humor. Dark, macabre humor. Homesickness, fear, death, all of the things we had been so worried about are now things we joke about. The danger in learning how to deal with war is that you become inured to the bad things. You get comfortable with them, and you find a new normal. That's dangerous because you can't trust war. War only takes from you. It may not take your life, but it takes a part of you and turns it into something else - something you can't explain or describe. Now it's just who you are.

I know that one day, we will look back and see that this was our Vietnam or our WWII, and that it didn't take a draft to bring us here.

This war has been going on for so long now most people have forgotten that it's even happening every day. I think that unless you know someone who is serving, wars truly aren't that big of a deal. I also think during every war in the past, those who were not directly affected by the war of their time have slowly forgotten it is even going on.

Four months have passed since the mortar strike. The next night, I learned that a unit from Camp Liberty lost a guy in the attack. No one really knew about it because unless someone was injured or killed in your unit or a sister unit, you didn't really hear much about it. We got to work that morning and Sergeant Major Williams told the four of us who worked in our shop that we had an important project today. We really had no clue what it could've been. We usually already had our projects laid out a couple weeks ahead of time. Then he told us we were going to build a shadow box for the soldier who was killed the night before. The mood in the shop reflected Sergeant Major Williams's mood that day. He is a very sentimental guy who really takes any loss as a personal loss. So, we built the shadow box and placed the name of Paul E. Andersen of Dowagiac, Michigan, beneath his picture. You don't really feel anything. You take what happens and move on. The 10 months, though, seemed even further away.

6

There is no hunting like the hunting of man, and those who have hunted armed men long enough and liked it, never care for anything else thereafter."

– Ernest Hemingway

WHEN I AM HOME ON LEAVE DURING THANKSGIVING, I run into a guy I went to high school with. He says, "You've changed a little, man. Seems like you've put 30 years of age onto a 25-year-old body."

I laughingly reply, "Well, I hope you're not calling me fat, 'cause that wouldn't be very nice."

But I know what he means. I carry myself differently, more confidently, and I have zero time or tolerance for bullshit.

Sometimes lessons you learn as a child have more meaning when you become an adult. I remember when I was nine, my stepdad had borrowed a wooden extension ladder from my grandpa. I was in the process of building a treehouse and needed a ladder. I found that wooden extension ladder in the shed by our house. I put it against the tree and realized it was going to be too long, and it would go higher than the treehouse I was planning to build. I decided the only way to make this work was to cut that ladder in half with a hatchet. My stepdad found the ladder cut in half propped up against that tree and made me call my grandpa to tell him what I had done. I cried and cried, begging my stepdad not to make me call. I remember crying on the phone telling my grandpa what had happened. He forgave me, but that memory has resonated with me for so many years because of the lesson I learned – decisions have consequences. I think about it again tonight at the bar with these friends from high school. I reflect on all the things I have done in Iraq and wonder if I made the right decisions and what consequences they wrought for others. While my friends and I are having a good time, part of me feels guilty. Part of me is still in Iraq.

7

I WENT HOME FOR TWO WEEKS, and the welcome home at the Dallas airport was more than anything I could've ever asked for. I knew what they did there prior to getting to Dallas, so I prepared myself mentally for this. I had watched a video that was on CNN about the veteran that set all of this up and welcomed soldiers home at the Dallas and Atlanta airports. As I departed the plane, I came through security, and as I turned the corner, I heard the cheers from what seemed to be a thousand people. I felt my throat swell up, and I turned around pretending to be searching for something, but I really wasn't prepared for it.

The older ladies standing at the opening of this long hallway were looking at me, and I felt a sigh of relief. I turned around, and I got that feeling of butterflies and nervousness in my stomach, that I thought I could only feel performing on stage. There were elementary kids, veterans; my uncle from Dallas was right at the front waiting for me. I gave him a hug and proceeded through the line full of handshakes, hugs, and tears. I had just spent 13 hours on a plane wanting nothing more than to just be home, and dreading the trip from Dallas to Kansas City. To see the veterans from past wars – WWII, Desert Storm, Vietnam, and some from the war in Iraq lined up single file on either sides of red stanchions cheering and waving made me realize that people really do give a shit about what we are doing. The whole world may not be concerned that a war is going on in Iraq, but here in Dallas, this group of men and women who have done exactly what we are doing right now took the time out of their lives to show up and tell us thank you. I felt pride and a sense of belonging. As I made my way through the line, I reached the end and saw an older man standing there wearing a hat that said "WWII Veteran." That's when I cried.

I've always had a profound respect for the men and women who fought during WWII and sometimes feel as if I were born during the wrong war time. The older man and I exchanged a very strange look, like we were looking at a reflection of each other in a mirror. It seemed as though we had known each other for years. I hugged him, and he cried, and so did I. I was very overwhelmed. I didn't know his story and didn't know mine, but it seemed like a reunion.

I reached the end and stood there for a minute off to myself. People were handing out bags of cookies and small gifts left and right. Then I thought about all these people who haven't fought in a war who say, "Thank you for your service," or "We appreciate everything that you do." It's great to hear, but I know that they will never fully understand or be able to put themselves in our boots. In the same sense, two hours before I left for Kuwait, Sergeant Major Williams came up to me, gave me a hug, and said, "I appreciate everything you do here." That was the first time he had said anything like that to me, and that was exactly when I knew I was right on point and accomplishing exactly what I had set out to accomplish on a personal level and with my military career. To have someone of that rank tell you that they appreciate everything that you do is a whole other level of appreciation to someone in uniform. Then getting home later and trying to keep up that pride and sense of accomplishment with everything you do is a struggle, it gets washed away in the mundane that seems to be life in the United States. One minute, you're in Iraq saving the world, and the next you're in Hopkins, Missouri, and nothing has changed. This is supposed to be my time to relax, but all I can think about is getting back to Iraq. It's a paradox.

You don't realize until you reach certain points in your life the real impact someone before you has made, and it's a reminder that you must follow in the same footsteps and set the example for the same ones who look up to you today. I've written to a third-grade class in Iowa for my friend Megan. Then I remembered when my dad was deployed to Saudi Arabia during Operation Desert Storm that my kindergarten class wrote to him. I remembered the feeling of pride knowing that my dad was there fighting for our country, not knowing that some 20 years later that I would put boots on the same ground that he did. In his case, he was there fighting to liberate Kuwait, and for me, I was in Kuwait waiting to leave for Baghdad. From those days in kindergarten until now I feel as though that I had already started to plan my future, considering where I am now, and who I am now.

You never feel the same after you put the uniform on for the first time. You feel 10 feet tall and bulletproof, but you don't understand the complexity of what's about to happen. The uniform will mold to your body, but it will also mold you as a person. You go through countless hours of training wearing it. You deploy to Iraq and wear it every day, and when you take the uniform off and put on civilian clothes, you feel completely naked and vulnerable. In a sense, that feeling of invincibility doesn't go away. Instead you respect the comfort that it gives you, the strength that it gives you, and everything it stands for. I know not all of the kids in the class will have the same feeling that I did then I was that age. But one day there will be one that will look back and remember my writing them, and I know I will have made an impact. They may one day have to put boots on ground once again in the same place that my dad and I both have.

8

09 Jan. 2010

ANOTHER MORTAR ATTACK TODAY – but the first one that we've received in the morning in the six months that I've been here. Standing in the latrine, still half groggy from waking up, I hear the impact of the first mortar. I don't even think anything of it, then I hear the siren going off. I walk out onto the staircase in front of the latrine, and hear, "Incoming! Incoming! Incoming!"

I look around for a bunker to jump into, but there isn't one on either side, so I just stand there. Then I hear the impact of the second mortar, which seems to be about 100 meters from where I am. I stand there and look around, as if I just don't care anymore at this point. I am becoming immune to mortar attacks. They are beginning to happen more frequently at night, but it is just random that one is happening in the morning.

I have been hearing stories of how these mortar attacks are taking place. The terrorists place a block of ice in the mortar tube and then place a round on top of it. In the hot Iraqi sun, the ice melts rather quickly. I suppose if they placed it overnight, it would happen much more slowly. As the ice melts, the mortar round slowly slides closer to the firing pin. Once the ice is fully melted... *Boom!* The round goes in whatever direction the tube is pointed. This is the story I was told by some guys in another unit who had come across deserted mortar tubes. I don't know if it's true or not, but it sounds plausible.

As I stand there staring into the sky, hearing the whistle of the rounds coming in, I happen to look over to my left. Our buildings and bathrooms are trailer houses which are set one by one, end to end in a straight line. The trailers where we live are surrounded by 12-foot high concrete walls, which we call T walls or Bremer walls. They protect us from mortars or any flying shrapnel that might be caused by a mortar. As I stand there and look over to my left, I see what I think is a rabbit. The confusing part is, this goddamn rabbit has antlers, and I think I am starting to lose my mind. I do a double take, and a triple take, in order to make any sense of what is happening. I stand there staring as mortar rounds come pouring in closer and closer, and all I can do is stare at this rabbit that has antlers, as though the rabbit is saying, "Focus on me." After a few minutes, the rabbit runs off. To where, I have no idea, but probably somewhere back into my imagination because to this day, I have not seen another antlered rabbit. But when he ran off, the mortar attack was over. I was exhausted, and I wasn't sure whether or not I'd been saved by a rabbit.

When the rounds are incoming, it's hard to comprehend what exactly is the right thing to do. You can jump in a bunker, but it seems that it's a little unnecessary because you're still in an opening, and in case of a direct hit, you would be blown to pieces anyway. Also, when people don't want to walk all the way to the latrine at night, they pee in the bunkers. I never have felt like I was going to die as much as I have today. I've felt an overwhelming sense of loss most of the day. Every vehicle I see with an Iraqi behind the wheel makes me uneasy, and I feel extremely vulnerable. There's got to be a reason for all of these strange things to have happened at once. I'm not a nervous person by nature, but I am on edge the rest of the day.

After this morning, I know anything at all can happen at any given moment. I don't feel as if I would be any safer back home, though. I think this uneasiness would follow me wherever I would go. Like a fly stuck on flypaper, I'll buzz and buzz trying to escape, hold the will to survive within myself, and the inevitable will still eventually happen. I don't want it to happen here, though, and not for a very long time.

22 Jan. 2010

Life as I know it has ruptured, and I'm lost. Everyone is gone. 260th packed up and left about two weeks ago. All my friends are gone, and I'm left here with these new people I don't know or want to know. I've managed to get five Army Achievement Medals and have more medals on the way. I just don't know anymore. Life is slowing down and my thirst for home is growing. I'll be there soon enough, and as soon as I'm there, I'll wish I were back here in Iraq.

PVT Martinez crosses my path. I am in the latrine when this guy came in. I was just getting out of the shower when he asked me if I had any ibuprofen. I tell him yes, in my room. As we walk, I can tell something is bothering him. He seems agitated. His hands are shaking, and he seems like he's in a hurry. He introduces himself, and I ask what unit he is with. He says 212 PSD team. He provides security for a colonel. His convoy had been hit with an IED yesterday. Today, his NCO had been shot by a sniper. He tells me that after all the adrenaline has worn off, his head is killing him. I listen, but something tells me not to ask too many questions. I understand he just needs to talk, so I just walk beside him and listen. When we get to my room, I give him the ibuprofen, and he leaves. I walked back into my room and closed the door. I sit there and think about all the problems I have and the shit I complain about, and in this moment, I realize they don't matter. There are bigger things to worry about. Soldier are dying here, and I'm sitting on an FOB safe from the world of Operation Iraqi Freedom.

Machen always reminds when we talk that we are FOBBITS, and that we truly don't do anything but wait out our time to go home. I cry for the first time in a long time, not enough to release all the fear and frustration, but I do feel a little better. I am just ready to go home. It has been a long 11 months. I just need to make it a little bit longer. Once I get home, I can let all of my feelings out privately.

When you think of home now, it's such a distant place because you've made this place your home. You look out the plane window down at the United States as you pass over, and the pilot says, "We're about to cross over into the east coast of America. Welcome home, soldiers." Then that overwhelming feeling takes over, and you just want to get the whole thing over with. The training, the deployment, the flight it all just needs to be over.

16 May 2010

Today we make a trip to Saddam Hussein's "Victory of America" palace. This place is crazy. It reminds me of visiting an abandoned house in the country back home. Nothing has really moved or changed since the day that we bombed it and Marines came through and cleared the palace.

As the story goes that we are told today, President Bush gave Saddam 48 hours to leave Iraq. Saddam decided to hold a meeting with his cabinet members to discuss what exactly to do regarding the news that he had received from President Bush about eight hours prior. President Bush received this information, and in order to kill Saddam Hussein, he ordered the USS Bunker Hill (CG-52) to fire tomahawk missiles on the Ba'ath Party house located on the same grounds of the palace. As Saddam pulled up to the palace to meet with some 250 men in the building, it was attacked with tomahawk missiles.

The attack killed all those who were in the meeting room. The funny part is that when Army engineers came through later to clear the building, they found a copy of *Pretty Woman* still in the DVD player that could've possibly been playing as these guys died.

The whole building is pretty eerie; a lot of death took place here. You walk around, and everything is destroyed. Chairs are still where they were left the day the bombs were dropped. The room where Dan Rather held his interview with Saddam Hussein in 2003 has been stripped clean. The pools that are inside the palace have blood stains still on their walls where an execution had taken place shortly before the bombs dropped. The pools weren't used for swimming, they were used for easy clean up after torturing someone in them.

The whole palace is surrounded by water, and I've been told that some crazy looking fish have been pulled out of its waters. The water came from the city of Baghdad. Saddam cut off the water supply to the city for eight days in order to fill the lake that surrounds the palace. He was just an all-around, fucked up guy. There is a mural of Saddam Hussein still up the road, and it's the last one that is still standing of him. I imagine one day I'll probably see that mural in history books and remember what it was like to stand beside it. As fucked up as everything is, I suppose it's a part of history, and it will hold its place.

17 Jul. 2010

I am home. Finally, my time in the desert is over. My family picks me up and takes me home. It feels good to be back with them. I haven't slept in three days, and last night, I thought I was having a heart attack. I started to panic, and my heart started to race as I sat in the living room with my mom and my sister. I couldn't calm down. My heart was beating out of my chest, and my mom got really concerned. She called my aunt, who's been a nurse for 20 years. She asked if I had taken any medications. I hadn't. She suggested that they take me to the emergency room. My mom drove me to the hospital, and I just remember them saying that my vitals were through the roof and trying to calm me down. They asked me if anything traumatic had happened recently. I said I had just gotten back from Iraq yesterday. They asked when the last time I slept was, and I said three days ago. I had been up and unable to sleep due to all of the excitement of going home and seeing my family that I had just simply forgot to sleep. They gave me a prescription for Ambien, and I took one before I left. As we were driving home, all of the colors from the street lights started to blend together. Mom said when we got home, she had to hold me up so I could pee. She also said that I was fast asleep on the couch, and as she hit the bolt on the door to lock it, I shot up off the couch out of a dead sleep and started looking for my weapon. What the fuck is happening to me? This is supposed to be a good thing that I came home, not a fucking nightmare.

It's been over a year and a half now since I've been back from Iraq. The nightmare did eventually end. It took about six months for me to fully get back into the swing of life in garrison. I am thankful for all of my friends and fellow soldiers. We talk about Iraq from time to time. The stories come to life every time I sit down with an old friend from the deployment and talk about our lives during that year. They come to life through random text messages with lyrics to songs that we would listen to over and over again while deployed or a stand-up comedian whom we listened to over and over again.

Last week, I was in the reenlistment office talking to the staff sergeant who was impatiently waiting for me to sign my next contract for another three years of active duty. The moment seemed as though it would go on forever, as time does when signing any contract. Army contracts are a little different from a contract on a car loan, though, because you're volunteering yourself and not your money. While this may seem a mundane task for a reenlistment NCO, it was a big deal to the guy who was signing the papers. I thought of the people I work with directly who would deploy to Afghanistan next year whether I was on that C-130 flying into a combat zone or not. I chose to do this because this is who I am. This is my calling and what I have grown to love in the past three and a half years, and I couldn't sit at home and think about how they would go without me. I signed the contract and let out a sigh of relief. I was proud of myself and the decision I had made to continue. Once again though, I will step foot into an unknown country, but this time, it's a more familiar place. The army is the same wherever you go.

I remember those first days heading to Iraq and the fear and anxiety I was feeling. I had looked around at the faces of the NCOs and specialists who had been here before, and they were at ease. This time I know I will be that guy who was sitting there at ease – almost like I am going home. There are so many things to be thankful for and so many more people to be thankful for in my life, especially Brittany. I want to protect them so that this will never happen here where we live today.

Ernest Hemingway once said, "If you're lucky enough to have lived in Paris as a young man, then wherever you go for the rest of your life, it stays with you, for Paris is a moveable feast." I feel the same way about deployments and anywhere we as humans feel attached to or guarded by, and that could be anything. That could be in the arms of someone you love or in a home that you built with your bare hands. Maybe it's dark and macabre, but I find serenity in fighting to protect those whom I love.

Afghanistan

Part 1

29 May 12

S O ANOTHER STORY BEGINS. I'm sitting in my room at Fort Riley not even a quarter of a mile from where I left the first time to go overseas. This time feels different. Strangely enough, I feel like I'm going home. I left my family two days ago at Mozingo Lake, where I planned a surprise birthday party for Brittany that was disguised as my going away party. I felt detached, as if I was preparing myself already for being gone for nine months straight. It's strange how that works, but you start to mentally prepare yourself for the deployment ahead. I sort of felt sorry for them that they worried so much about my leaving. That's what families do, though, they worry so you don't have to. There really is nothing to fear on a large scale, because I would be more likely to get killed living in a major city in the United States than I would in Afghanistan.

A person who hasn't experienced war doesn't really understand that mostly it's just boring. I guess the idea of someone going to war is a lot different to a person who hasn't experienced it. I do understand their general concern for me, but I assured them that I would be fine, and I wasn't worried about leaving. I fear the flying around eastern Afghanistan in a Blackhawk, a definite rolling target. I keep telling myself that I signed up for this. I'm going overseas once again, and this time, I volunteered. I could've just walked away from the Army, but I didn't, and that is my motivation.

The first time, hours before I left, I was crying in my room – a brand new soldier going to Iraq. As I stood in the parking lot and told my family goodbye, my mom started crying. I kissed her on the forehead and said I would be okay. As she walked away, I stepped over to my grandpa and asked him to take care of her. She had recently quit smoking, and I knew this would put a lot of stress on her. I worried she would pick up that habit again. I didn't want to cry in front of her because I knew it would be added stress on her. I saved it until I got back to my room.

This time there are no tears. This time, it's Afghanistan, and I'm telling Brittany goodbye. I feel as though she is prepared for my leaving since we have been talking about it a lot recently. I've been overseas before, and I'm surer of myself this time around. I feel better about deploying because I will be going with Chief Sprague, Cottrill, Leibengood, and SSG Rich, all of whom I had been working with for six months. My confidence reassured her – a confidence I didn't have when I left for Iraq. Leaving for that first deployment, everything was new, and I was reactive rather than proactive in dealing with my emotions. I let them get the best of me. Not this time.

Once you've been somewhere with the Army, it's all going to be the same, no matter where you go. I understand that now. I think that's why active duty is a better option than the National Guard or Reserves. The army is already your home on active duty, and your life day in and day out is the Army, so nothing really changes except working seven days a week instead of five. I really don't know what to expect from the country, and I think that's the beauty of it all. I'm excited to see all of the eastern part of Afghanistan and write and take as many pictures as possible. This will be another year of soul searching.

31 May 12

First day in Kyrgyzstan. We landed at Manas transfer center. It reminds me a lot of Kuwait, but there is a bar, and the post is a lot smaller than Camp Buehring was in Kuwait. It looks like a scene straight out of a Vietnam movie. We actually have beds this time and not cots, though, and clean sheets, so I can't complain much. The clean sheets only hide the atrocities that most likely have happened on the mattress underneath. But I try not to think about that and to just be glad I have a bed.

I miss Brittany a lot, and I didn't think it would bother me as much, but it really does.

You can see the mountains right outside the perimeter. There are so many beautiful things here, but we're stuck behind the fence unable to enjoy any of it. I'll start lifting tomorrow. Just like the last deployment, I'm going to hit the gym hard and cut some weight before I get home. It's crazy to think just a few hours ago we were sitting in Kansas, and now we're about 11 hours ahead of that time, yet the world is still turning back home just like it is here. That's the thing about deployments, though. We leave, and time doesn't stop back home. The toothpaste and the deodorant I bought is from Walmart in Maryville, and that Walmart is in full swing. It's about 1:00 in the afternoon there. Billy the stockman is pushing carts, and I'm in Kyrgyzstan going to war again. I still would rather be here than there. I used to work at Walmart many years ago, and to picture what life would be like if I were still pushing carts makes it easier for me to say that I would rather be here going off to war.

We have rollover training tomorrow around 1400. Rollover training consists of practicing how to get out of a Humvee if you ever found yourself in a rollover accident. I'm hoping we're leaving here within the next three days on our way to Bagram in Afghanistan. Then within the next week, we'll be in Sharana. I will be flying around eastern Afghanistan fixing weapons, a job I really hate. I don't know what I'm doing, and the uncertainty of the job is making it not so enjoyable. I think if I knew more about fixing weapons, I would feel better. Maybe in the next few months I will get more comfortable with it. Stay positive, right? I wish I could just travel around and write stories about the different areas that I venture to. I could see myself as an Army journalist. That would be perfect. That's just not in the cards right now, that's for sure.

1 Jun. 12

The mountains are beautiful here. I could be staring at them one second, and the next second, my thoughts are disrupted by a conversation between two guys coming out of Afghanistan talking about how it's gonna work the lazy out of us for sure. I started back at the gym today, and it felt great. My schedule with the gym and eating and sleeping are going at the same rate they were the first time I left for Iraq, and I couldn't be more pleased. Sergeant Miller told me today that I look like I'm always ready to kill someone. Ha! Far from it. Usually, I'm calm on the outside, but the wheels are turning on the inside. I may look pissed off, but I rarely am. I guess it's just how my face looks.

I fell asleep in the afternoon and had a dream that I was in a restaurant back home fighting and wrestling with a guy I went to high school with. When I realized that we'd get the cops called on us, I told him we should get out of here. So, I left the restaurant and found myself on the streets of the Plaza in Kansas City. Like many dreams, I found myself moving sluggishly as I made my way onto the steps of a fountain in downtown Kansas City. I turned around to see what looked like a huge buffalo. I was terrified and tried to make my way up the steps and turned to see a smaller one was right beside me. Then I woke up. I went outside and felt drained of life, like I didn't have a drop of water in my body and hadn't eaten in days. As I stepped out the door, I realized I was still in Afghanistan, and Brittany was still very far away. I felt the onset of loneliness come over me, and I felt homesickness hit me in the gut. The feel of her touch, her smile, and that caring look in her eyes that would put me at ease... I miss her so much, and it's only been a few days. I pulled out a sweatshirt of hers that she sent with me. She had sprayed it with her perfume, and I put it in a Ziploc bag to be sure it never lost its smell. I put it to my face and breathed her in for a few seconds, and put it back into its bag. For a moment, I felt better. I did some research on the meaning behind encountering buffalo in a dream, it's a sign of survival and that you should pay attention to the path you're following in your life. That's probably a good sign, right? She was my reason to survive, and I had to stay strong every day of these nine months because I promised her that I would come home safe and sound.

The realization of where I am set in today. There was a thunderstorm around 2030. I was in the tent when I heard the thunder hit. It sounded like a mortar similar to the ones you encounter in Iraq. I thought of all those nights we'd get mortared at Camp Liberty and how thankful I felt to be alive. The cool air passed through the tent and for the time being cleared out the smell of dirty socks and underwear. I laid on my back and stared at the roof of the building. The thunder continued and it was calming, and the smell of rain passing through the tent. We were far away from any mortar, and I knew I could relax.

Mortars can take a strong man and make him very weak real quick. There's just nothing that compares to those feelings of "close calls."

Since returning from Iraq our unit has had several people pass away, either from suicide or car accidents. I just want to make it home this time and feel normal once I get there, and not find myself in a situation where I feel ending my life is the only way out. I have too much to lose this go around. I do feel confused and wonder exactly why our unit from Iraq had so many tragedies happen. I don't know if this is common after a deployment or not. Regardless, it's a damn shame.

2 Jun. 12

We made it to Bagram Air Force base in Afghanistan this afternoon. The sleeping conditions weren't horrible. We were in a huge, round tent. It reminded me of the coverall tarp buildings my stepdad and uncle used to build when I was a kid. At the end of the building were two very large openings that would let in a cross breeze. The only unforgiving part about that tarp and wind is that if you were standing near that tarp when the wind kicks up, it would crack down on you like a whip. Many times, I witnessed guys get whipped in the ass by that tarp as they were trying to hurry in. While it was definitely funny, I did not want to fall victim to the crack of the tarp whip.

I went and ate then came back and tried to sleep, but it was so hot, I woke up with my mouth dry after about an hour. Everyone I travelled to Afghanistan with is so spread out in this tent. My buddies and I did our best to try and find bunks near each other, but it didn't happen right away. Some guys finally got a flight out of Bagram and headed to their base in Afghanistan for nine months. I was able to acquire a bunk closer to the other guys once those guys cleared out. We didn't argue over who would get the top or bottom bunk. The struggle was in finding a bunk that was close to a wall outlet where you could charge a computer to watch movies or your iPod.

There are mountains surrounding this entire place, and it's windy as hell. There are big-ass rocks to walk on just like in Iraq. I'm waiting to step wrong and break my ankle. Between that and numerous blisters on my feet from these shitty Nike boots I bought back at Fort Riley, I've mainly just tried to stick to my bunk.

5 Jun. 12

We're still in Bagram. I'm just hitting the gym and trying to keep my mind occupied. I slept a full night for the first time last night. This morning when I came back from the gym, an overwhelming emptiness came over me. I was thinking when I get home, I probably won't be able to sleep in the same bed as Brittany for the first week because I'll still be in that alert phase that you go through right after a deployment. I miss her a lot, and she's on my mind constantly. I'm ready to get out of here and start working and doing something to keep my mind busy. The gym is great and keeps me occupied, but it's only for an hour or two out of the day, and unfortunately, even Afghanistan has 24-hour days.

They've got us taking doxycycline once a day now to combat the chance of getting malaria. I have about three million pills, so that should be enough to last me nine months. I love when the Army shoves pills at you and says, "Take this." Saying no is not an option. I have a feeling that this deployment is going to be a lot different than the last. I'm going to have a lot more to write about, that's for sure. I feel as though traveling around the country and seeing this beautiful scenery will cause the words to flow naturally. I'm going to start documenting my dreams, which have been strange lately. I'm going to try and piece some things together and see what they mean. I don't want to go home empty and lost like the last time.

Before I left, my dad told me that I need to take some "me" time once I get back to adjust. Last time, I ended up in the emergency room with a panic attack because I didn't ease myself back into the civilian life. I come alive when I'm gone, and when I get home, things become chaotic again. I'm left wondering where that motivated, optimistic person I'd been during the deployment went. Live and learn though, and I think since I'm aware this time, things will be a lot different, and I'll have my shit together.

7 Jun. 12

The 68th anniversary of D-Day was yesterday. I can't help but feel that they had it much worse than we have it now. You always feel more patriotic when you're deployed. I was thinking to myself that back then they were fighting for ground that would eventually lead to the fall of Nazi Germany. We're fighting for the fall of the Al-Qaeda? I used to think that once we killed Osama bin Laden that things would start to change, but it really didn't make a difference. I think this war has lost its purpose. I think every regular Joe that deploys isn't really sure exactly what he's supposed to accomplish. At least when my friends and family ask, I have no idea what to tell them.

Right now, I still feel like I appreciate the experience. To wake up in the morning and see the mountains outside, to spend this time soul searching. At times, I feel as if Afghanistan or anywhere else I'm deployed is the better place to be. I can't tell the world stories of days in Iraq or Afghanistan if I don't experience them first, but I am starting to wonder if these stories even matter at all. Do people actually find any interest in these stories, or am I just writing myself a textbook to use in future deployments? I learned so much from returning from the last deployment that I will use this time. Just learning how to keep myself and my mind occupied with writing and the gym have made a world of difference. Routine is definitely crucial in keeping my mind at ease.

We still have yet to reach Sharana, but we will be leaving tomorrow night at 2000. I believe it's going to be a very dull and boring deployment, so I will have to find ways to keep it interesting. This won't be like Baghdad where we were getting attacked every other night. The only reason I want to go home now anyway is to see Brittany. If I didn't have her as my reason to return home, I would say leave me here in Afghanistan until the war was finally over.

Even though I miss my family, things get more complex with the Internet available. I understand that our families want to keep in touch with us, and it's probably selfish of me to think so, but being so connected by technology becomes a distraction. I would rather not have the distractions. I think deployments would be much easier if we were shut off from the world.

8 Jun. 12

We finally get a flight to FOB Sharana in the Paktika province of Afghanistan. This will be home for the next nine months. Unfortunately, when we arrive, the old unit we are replacing is still moving out, so space is limited, and we've had to resort to sharing rooms with other guys. I'm so tired I barely find the energy to write this, all of the traveling and the altitude is really taking it out of me. I'm staying in Cottrill's room for what I believe is the night, but who knows. He has a twin bed, which of course would be too small for both of us, so I made a bed out of duffel bags and rucksacks on the floor to keep from sleeping on the cold concrete. I hate it here. I really do. I imagine this feeling will be temporary but at the moment that's how I feel. I just want to rewind and be back at Brittany's parents' house, sleeping in her bed. I just miss her so much. I may have volunteered for a two-week job tearing down another COB, which would mean a two-day drive through Afghanistan. The thought scares the hell out of me the more I think about it. Flying through Afghanistan is one thing, but driving just seems like asking for trouble. I may have gotten ahead of myself when I agreed to be a part of that.

21 Jun. 12

This place is not much different from Iraq. The scenery doesn't change and neither does the dust or clouds of shit from the burn pits swirling through the air. We've been working a lot with the Special Forces guys here. They said a local national that was a taxi driver during the beginning of the war got in good with them. When some of the Taliban killed some of the SF guys in the beginning of the war with an IED, the guy knew who planted it. So, he went to their house and gunned them down. Now every time this local national does work with them, he rolls out with one of the weapons he took from the guys he killed that planted the IED. The SF guys talk so casually about death, and I can't help but feel closer to danger with every story they tell me. It's all pretty fascinating.

I head out tomorrow around 0630 to COB Margah. I still have yet to find it on an actual map, but it can't be too far away. My body is starting to adjust to the stress from being here emotionally and physically. The terrain is pretty demanding, and so is the altitude. I struggled with homesickness the first few days, but now I am finally starting to come around. I just needed a little time to find my groove and get down a routine.

They caught a guy drawing a map of our town square. He was a forklift driver, and I don't think it's not just another attempt at suicide bombers. I feel like there is more going on, as though they may be planning a larger attack. Suicide bombers cause mass confusion for a short amount of time, kind of a like shooting a BB gun at a bear – you're only going to piss it off. A larger, more organized attack would cause more damage on a greater scale. We have also worked with the Polish commandos. Chief has gotten to know them pretty well, and I'm glad we could be of assistance. The Polish guy was telling me that they couldn't fly into Ghazni Province because the Taliban was shooting the helicopters every time they flew in. They put a hold on all flights except American military flights into the area. Ghazni is kind of the wild west of Afghanistan, and I know at some point we will be travelling there, but I'm just not sure when yet.

22 Jun. 12

Chief, SSG Rich, and I flew to Margah today. Talk about landing on the moon. The soldiers knew we weren't from that COB and looked at us like they hadn't seen human life for years. They were out here by themselves overlooking the village of Margah. Pakistan was just a few short miles away just over the mountain range to our east, which I was told was the Hindu Kush mountain range. I haven't been able to verify that yet from a credible resource. We got to work early when we got there and finished putting safeties on three 50 cal. machine guns. The last two were at the top of a mountain at an outpost overlooking the numerous valleys that surrounded the COB. We went with SGT Dyson, who was the unit armorer, and he led us to the ECP, which was a big steel door, and as soon as you passed through it, there were these barriers with concertina wire surrounding us in an arch over our heads.

Dyson locked and loaded his M4, and we followed his lead. We followed a trail to where the HESCO barriers ended, and we officially entered the game. We were now no bullshit a part of this war. That was the most satisfying feeling I had felt in a long time. We hit the bottom of the mountain and started our way up. It was three hundred feet high, and we were hurting, stopping numerous times dealing with the change in altitude. We thought that 300 feet would be no problem, but it was kicking our asses. We had about 65 pounds of extra gear on at the time, and every step was a struggle. It took us about 15 minutes, and we finally made it to the top.

We had walked into Vietnam. The Afghan National Army soldiers used sandbags and made huts out of them. They had a goat tied
up outside their makeshift fort, and when I asked what it was for, I
was told it was for milk until that runs out, and then it's for meat.
There was wire and nails and everything else to get cut on. It was a
horrible mess, but these boys called it home, and I felt a lot of respect
for that.

We took about two hours to take apart and clean the 50 cal. That
and M4s were these guys' only defense against any attackers who
might attempt to take the OP. Surrounding the mountain were numerous claymore mines. The clacker sat resting in the sun on a sandbag inside the tower overlooking the largest of the valleys. It was good
that we had come up here because if the guys that lived up there had
needed to use that 50 cal., it might've shot one round but would've
jammed immediately after. After we got it cleaned up, I fired a few
rounds through the 50 cal. into the side of a mountain, just to make
sure it worked. After that, we made our way down the mountain. We
jumped on the chopper just in time to avoid an attack that was planned
later that evening by Al Qaeda forces hiding out the neighboring village. They almost didn't let us go, but we boarded the helicopter and
headed to our home away from home, back to Sharana.

24 Jun. 12

We would never know what it was like to leave home behind. We
would always have a way to communicate back with the lives that we
left. This would hinder some of us but many needed it. I looked at
that connection as a crutch. All of the distractions of living in the
United States, the internet, cell phones, all of those means of communication – I wanted to experience life without all of those distractions. I don't regret that I am able to keep in touch with everyone,

but we are young men on an adventure exploring the world. We don't need to have ties to everything that we have known our entire lives leading up until this point. Call me selfish, but a part of me longed to leave it all behind if only for nine months. If we were to come here and separate ourselves, I believe that would make for a more meaningful story. I want pen to paper, boot to ground, and to really grind out these nine months and see just what happens. I feel we would appreciate the journey that much more.

I didn't feel guilty from time to time when I would play dumb and tell everyone back home that the Internet was down. I just didn't care to give everyone progress updates on daily life. Yes, it is true that we hate it here while we are here at times, but that taste of near death and feeling of the long meaningful days have filled our cups to the brim. Now I am fully invested in this deployment. The brotherhood I've developed with Chief Sprague, SSG Rich, Cottrill, and

Leibengood is extremely important, and this is exactly where my focus needs to be at this point in the deployment.

Some here with us now will never experience a mortar attack, and the ones who have are praying for that whizzing rain to fall somewhere among us. I miss the adrenaline rush; it made for many great stories. This war, this pathetic excuse for a war, is draining that glass. It's become my final season without a Super Bowl ring. I don't think I can articulate to anyone back home what being here means to me. I am on a path of self-discovery, and I want to see who I really am and what I'm made of. I don't feel as though I would be able to explain the importance of that concept to another person.

"The hands always remember the rifle." It's not that way for me. I will always remember living without life's amenities and having to survive here without handing over my sanity. It's the beauty of seeing what I am made of. That's what makes us stronger, and that's where the good stuff lives.

30 Jun. 12

Today was kind of a big day. I asked Brittany's parents if they would be all right with me marrying her. Her dad's response was fitting for the situation because all he said was, "How big is the herd of goats that you would be willing to trade for her?"

This was a big relief. I had been thinking about this off and on for quite some time and now the plan is actually being put into action. Her parents and I are talking now about getting the ring made by a jeweler back home. I am thinking it will cost around $5,000. I have put quite a lot of money away since being in Afghanistan, and this will be worth every penny. I don't plan to say anything to her of course. I will just keep letting her talk to me about a future wedding we will plan to have.

2 Jul. 12

We make it to FOB Lightning, which is a little further north of where we were in Sharan. The flight isn't bad at all. We arrive at Lightning, hop in a truck, and are taken to a room where there is an Afghan colonel. He serves us chai tea and offers us a plateful of sugar-coated almonds, fruit snack things, as well as other goodies. He talks with us about the weapons class we are going to teach to his soldiers, and we all just make small talk. All of the Afghan people that I have met have been very welcoming and are all-around great people. After speaking with the colonel, we teach a weapons class to some of the Afghan Army guys all while working with an interpreter who does his best to explain what we are saying, so these guys will understand. They are all very polite. They pick up quickly on the M16A2 and are just all-around happy people. I thought I would feel awkward around them, but I feel very comfortable. As they are filing out, each one shakes my hand. I couldn't help but think that after we leave, half these guys won't survive the first few months. They smile now and are content, and that's all that matters.

Walking back from the classroom, I see the ruins where Alexander the Great had an outpost. Crazy to believe that stuff has been standing since 330 BC. The colonel told us that the United States still uses that as an OP today. He said it's run down and isn't much, but it's a great location to overlook the village below. Alexander the Great once waged war here against Persia, and that's all the information you need to know in order to understand just how long war has been going on in this country. The colonel tells us that we cannot convoy outside the wire to visit the ruins without the United States base commander's authorization. He says that won't happen though because the road leading to the OP is littered with roadside bombs, and the last thing he wants is to feel responsible for the deaths of American soldiers. I told Chief, "Well, at least we asked."

There is one funny thing about deployments. No matter where you travel to, it seems there is always a Korean lady giving massages in some run-down building on a post no matter where you go. Chief said we should go and get a massage, and I wasn't about to turn that down. We get to this building, and there is a line of chairs against a wall. We sat down and told the lady that we wanted a massage, and she said it's $20 for an hour. Now take into consideration that I've never stepped foot in a massage parlor even in the United States, so this foreign country I was in just went to a whole new level of foreign for me. This cute girl comes out of the back room and takes Chief to another room in the back. There are plywood walls, so you hear everything that's going on in this building. I'm waiting to go back and an older lady comes in and says, "Come, come." I didn't know what to think. She led me to this room that had a cot with a towel over the top. She kind of nods and walks out, I'm extremely confused about the rules of what's going to take place. So, I start to undress but I'm about to have a panic attack because I'm not sure if this is clothed or what's supposed to happen. Just when I'm about to reach the realm of my comfortability in the situation she walks in, and I'm standing there with my shirt off and pants undone. She looks at me for a few seconds, and there's an awkward silence, and all I said was, "I'm not sure what to do."

I hear from the other side of the plywood wall Chief laughing and yelling, "Take your clothes you idiot."

All in all, after I got it figured out it, was a great massage. It was a good laugh, too.

I went out last night. You could hear a mass of children playing just outside the wire. Their laughter somehow put me at ease, and for a while, I felt relaxed. Earlier in the evening, I had lost my wallet, which had left me in a bit of panic. I finally located it when on the loudspeaker they called out, "SPC Rucker, please report to Mayor Cell for a lost item." I got my wallet back, but only after I did 30 burpees in front of two guys I'd never met before.

Tonight, when I go out the children's laughter has subsided, and all I can hear is barking dogs. There's a full moon, and you can still see the outline of the mountains. This FOB is a blackout FOB, so there are no lights on at night so as to keep from giving away our position. It's really peaceful when all of the lights are out. You can see every star the night sky has to show. This reminds me of nights on my grandparents' farm in Blockton, Iowa. My cousin and I would lie on the grass at night as kids and look up into the sky and look at all of the different galaxies and stars, and there wasn't a worry in the world.

4 Jul. 12

We got back to Sharana from FOB Lightning this morning. We lost our first soldier in the brigade. A PFC at Tillman was in a guard tower and was shot three times by a sniper, at least that's the story we were told. I'm sure the official report will come out later, but as of right now that's all the information we've been given. There was probably a package in the mailroom for him that will sit unclaimed. The mail clerk is sitting there looking at that package right now and thinking this guy will never get to see what was in it. There are parents at home on the 4th of July enjoying their day off with their family, and they have no clue at this moment that their son is dead.

Snipers are something no one can avoid because if a man has the will and the countless hours of training it takes to become a sniper, then the Average Joe will never know he was a target. Cottrill said that one of our towers got hit by sniper fire the other night. The Apaches went out and blew up everything in the direction the round came from. We watched the Salerno video of the ECP get blown up and the six Taliban that attempted to infiltrate FOB Salerno. Our guys really did a number on them and killed them all including the two Taliban guys that blew themselves up. No one outside was hurt on our side. I feel sorry for those parents getting the news today. It's just a sad story.

6 Jul. 12

In a war zone, you get used to having filthy hands. Your body adjusts to the dust, the sun, and your legs get used to the long walks. Your mind grows miles upon miles dealing with the lack of anything in between. There are no mile markers during a deployment, you only see a beginning and an end. We are here, and at some point, you realize you can't turn back. There's no going back to where you came from until someone says you're done. Here's to hope and struggle and those long miles that you walk in your head every day. Some of these miles you'll never forget. Like the names of those dead, killed in combat, and you wonder what they didn't do that day that got them killed. Did they make a mistake, or did they do something out of their routine, and the universe responded. It's the Afghan civilian you gave your blood to because he lost his legs in an explosion, only to find out the next day that he died anyway. My blood was in that man's body for a short period of time, and I never even knew his name. It's the people you respect and the ones you know you could never trust. It's a war zone, and you know you'll always want to see it again. War is an addiction, and for those of us who truly find value in it, nothing will ever be able to compare to it.

People show their true colors while deployed. Major Dick Winters once said, "War exposes the best and worst that are called to fight. I know of no man who lacked character in peace and then discovered character in combat." That quote is very true when it comes to deciding whom you can trust and whom you cannot while deployed. You figure out people within the first few weeks. Everyone is a hard charger until they feel the weight of nine months suddenly fall on their shoulders.

11 Jul. 12

Second day of tower guard. Yesterday, I watched a woman walk some goats near the fence line. As the day moved on, I stepped outside the tower to the base to stretch my legs. I spotted a silhouette on the horizon on top of a small hill which was directly in front of our M240 Bravo. I made myself a smaller target beside some HESCO barriers. My first thought was, this is a sniper, and he knows I'm down here and hadn't had time yet to pick me up in his scope before I spotted him. So, I walked around behind the tower and up the stairs back into our nest. I grabbed the binoculars and finally found the guy sitting on top of the hill watching the road on our blind side. He had his back towards us. He had no purpose out there, but we watched him for three hours before he moved. Cottrill's comment now has me paranoid that there are snipers all over these hills. That's why it would be so much easier to fight a uniformed military.

We sit here in this tower while the American people sleep. They get the option of advancing themselves daily, while our lives are at a standstill. I've watched 300 or some odd goats graze. The guy on the motorcycle rides back and forth right after lunch. I've thought a lot about my grandparents recently. These farmers out here remind me of them. They go to take care of the animals during the day and just mind their business. I wondered how my grandpa would feel if another military set up base right by his farm. He would probably be pissed and annoyed mostly. I imagine that's what these people are feeling about us. They just want their lives back and for us to be gone.

13 Jul. 12

Thoughts of war and war of thoughts.

Our war wasn't about body count. We were fighting a more premodern enemy with our more modern tactics. The guy who got killed, Mooseman, wasn't shot by a sniper. He had gone to check the body of a Taliban guy who they thought had been killed. When he approached, the guy was playing dead. He shot Mooseman once in the vest and twice in the face. This was what I was told today. The kid probably got his first kill and died all in the same day. He was 24 years old. Meanwhile, I'm here on my second deployment. Any of those mortars in Iraq could've killed me. The sleepless nights in Iraq boil down to the countless mortars that fell from the sky on us. Being on tower guard, staring at the miles of mountains for countless hours on end gives me a lot of time to think. It also brings back a lot of memories from Iraq. Ones that I hate. Of what I feared before I left to come here. The anxiousness and always being on high alert. I was scared to death of that place at times. The night in Iraq when we were on a sticks lane doing training and a mortar landed 50 feet from us and did not explode. It was a dud. That should've been my day to die, but it wasn't, and I'm not sure why I've been so lucky. There will always be hope that when death does come calling, it comes quickly, and there is no suffering involved.

13 Jul. 12

Brittany crosses my mind on a constant basis. I think of her touch, her scent, and the feel of her body wrapped inside mine. This love is a fire that will stay burning strong. It is as consistent as the thoughts of her in my mind. Yes, I am at war, but I keep her close to me at all times. I pull out her hoodie from the zip-lock bag from time to time just to get a reminder of her scent. I have stared death in the face. I have grown to learn that every man has his day in which the soul will leave the body and his vessel will be left behind. So many days have been longer than necessary, but I have learned to accept that and to embrace them as a friend and close companion. I feel as though I have unfinished business, and that's why I keep finding myself on these de-ployments. It's not that I lack the ability to say no and walk away from the Army, but something more powerful than myself is keeping me here because this is where I belong. That is what keeps a sniper round from entering my eye and spraying my very thoughts throughout the walls of this tower. In any case, with every man who dies, it happens unexpectedly, and they never believe it will be them. But for now, I wait like the rest of us – in oblivion – until the truth stops us dead where we stand.

Stephen Hawking once wrote, "The pope told me not to explore before the time of the big bang because that was God's time." Stephen Hawking explored it anyway. This is our time here in Afghanistan, and we are the gods protecting those who live amongst the goats and sheep. I won't let these times in our history go unrecorded or let them slip my mind prior to putting the pen to this paper. This is what will be read about in centuries to come. We are the Shakespeares of our time, and we must embrace that and not blindly ignore our position in history.

16 Jul. 12

The mountains can drive a man crazy after looking at them eight hours a day. They can make a man grow impatient and leave him angry at himself. You sit there for countless hours and stare into the nothingness of this valley, and you contemplate every life decision you ever made, and over time, it has a way of getting the best of you. My back is killing me, and it's getting old wearing this gear all the time. I've been daydreaming a lot about Brittany's and my wedding. The thought of proposing and our wedding, I believe, is making me grow impatient. I think we've decided to have it on a beach somewhere. Little does she know that I've already put those wheels in motion, and the ring should be ready shortly before I get back from Afghanistan.

17 Jul. 12

I know they're watching us. It's so easy for us to look for them. They've hit so many ECP's lately that eventually they'd hit ours. That fear wouldn't hit me until I was racked out late at night. We have gone too long without having any issues on Sharana. Eventually something will happen. Cottrill had too soft of a heart to realize if any of the local nationals had cruel intentions, and Leibengood just went with the flow. Chief Sprague and SSG Richardson agreed that we have gone too long without having any problems on our post. Every other post in the area had been hit at some point, and I was just wondering when it would be our turn. If anything, a war taught to you let go of most things you loved. In order to understand what you were doing, you had to let go of your thoughts as well. You had to put yourself in the mindset that everything around you could kill you at some point if it really wanted to. Life here seems like a dream at times, and you wonder if you will ever really wake up from the dream. Then you wake up sometime later, and you're home. It's almost as though the deployment never happened. One day you're in Afghanistan, and the next day you're in Fort Riley, Kansas. It all happens so suddenly that it really does seem like a dream.

1 Aug. 12

Today I watched two bodies blanketed in American flags carried through two separate lines of our soldiers. They were loaded up into Blackhawks which hovered above us for two minutes before they flew off. It was sad, but we still don't know who they were. The bodies seemed so small passing by us. We weren't told who they were, only where to be and what time. We're made to grow accustomed to death, and it's no longer confusing. As we stood there, I saw Cottrill sway back and forth and then hit the ground from the heat. He locked out his knees and the weight of his M249 just threw him on his back.

The guys behind him picked him up and dragged him to the med building, and we filled in his spot because that's what we do when we lose people. We fill their place. Just like we fill the void within ourselves that this place makes. Our shop sergeant leaves soon. He went to mental health and threatened suicide. I'm not sure of all the details, but I guess if he needs to go home, then so be it. I am to take his place. This is going to be a long seven months.

10 Aug. 12

We've been at Bande Sarde for three days now. We came here to gage some weapons. The loss of our shop SGT hasn't hindered us a bit. I think if anything it has brought us closer together, and I have worked more on my personal weaknesses. I have started to better control my sour moods and realize that my actions do control most of the shop's moods. There is no Internet here, so communication with Brittany has been minimal, but I do miss her more than I miss home. These barren COBs are a great place for a man to categorize his thoughts and play with them in great ways. Like I talked about earlier, the world at times can seem so big in the grand scheme of things. I think if you're able to find a way to shrink the size of your world down it's easier to manage. It has been easier now for me to work on the things I can change, and that is my mood. I know I haven't been sleeping the best, and in the full circle of things, that is probably what is affecting my mood.

We hear the outgoing 120 mm mortars shoot out to warn the terrorists planting IEDs that the next one will be your head if you don't vacate the premises. Still, even with the random explosions, life is quite simple and seems to be more meaningful. This does not absolve the random thoughts of death and not making it home. The first group of mortars sent out shook our building. That didn't make my heart skip a beat, but when Chief put the hammer to a piece of metal on the table, it sent my heart through the roof, and I was agitated for a while after that. I wasn't expecting it and was caught off guard. I still miss Brittany's voice and her colorful personality. I miss her and love her very much.

11 Aug. 12

Something came to mind today. We rise, and we restore ourselves. We venture among those in our lives. We take. We give because in order to crank a machine we must give. At the end of the day, that same machine gives out what we put in it. This lubricates our spirits and lifts us, and we become better products.

I love Brittany so much. Being able to say that and mean it is such a great feeling. This means that I am human after all, ha! Those I love who are close to me inspire me to be better and work hard, and it drives me to succeed. Where am I? I am where I am supposed to be, kicking in the doors with brute strength and grunting at whatever is on the other side. I may fail, but damn, I'll make a smart-ass comment on the way down.

25 Aug. 12

We finally got the call to go up to Ghazni. It was about a two-hour flight, and one of the worst ones yet. I hadn't been so nervous on a helicopter as I was today and was very happy when we finally landed. As we got off the helicopter and got settled in our tent, two Apaches flew over and blew the hell out of something just outside the wire. I know now what the Polish Commandos meant when they said that Ghazni is the wild west of Afghanistan. Whatever they were after, they must've killed it because there was a lot of cheering going on once it was over.

We set up shop in our tent and started working on some 120 mm mortars that needed annual services done. This place is pretty small, and we are pissing in PVC tubes and shitting inout houses. Yes, they still burn their shit here with diesel fuel. We worked pretty late into the night and only stopped to eat. Dinner was some cold bologna sandwiches and small bags of trail mix. Later, I went back to the chow tent to see if anything was left from dinner and found a stray cat sitting on the table eating what was left of the meat that was left out. I didn't help myself to another plate and hoped that the cat hadn't had his way with that meat before we did.

That was not the last that we would see of that cat that tonight. We turned out the lights about an hour ago. Chief was reading some Clive Cussler book wrapped up in his sleeping bag when I hear him yell, "What the fuck!" I pulled my head out of my sleeping bag and turned my headlamp towards his direction just in time to see that cat go flying out of the tent. It had somehow found his way into his sleep bag, and he had no clue. As he lay there reading his book, the cat started moving around at his feet. When he shot up off his cot, the cat went flying out of the tent screeching the whole way. I said at least you got to see a little action while out here, ha!

7 Sept. 12

The landscape has dug in. The mountains, the sand, the flights, the parts drawers, everything. Brittany's sister Kelsey dates a guy who is also in the Army. We are currently on the same post. I highly doubt I'll see him, though; our schedules just conflict too much. Oh well, five more months of this place, and it will be time to go home. I am ready for it. Afghanistan has taught me a lot about leadership. I think on the civilian side it will benefit me more, but here it really just amounts to babysitting. We're still flying around all of the time, but we're still at Sharana enough to go through parts drawers. Parts drawers have been our life for quite a while now.

> *This distance has absorbed the mass of waters in between*
> *And swollen are the words and our beliefs*
> *Yet we are fine*
> *You'll always remember this even with time*

8 Sept. 12

The scenery is beautiful here. I enjoy the blackout COPs because it gives you a chance to enjoy the stars and the nights themselves. This place, Bahghay, has some British India history dating back to 1838. The walls here are old and remind me that so many people have been here before us. There is a cave also in the side of a mountain that I would love to go into but know it will never happen. Still, I can daydream about all the awesome things I wish I could do, right?

12 Sept. 12

I depart on my first convoy today. I was talking to my mom about it last night. She wanted to remind me of when she used to sing to me when I was little. I actually remembered listening to her sing that to me. It put me at ease, especially when I was thinking about the 30-minute drive to the next post. It's just like a drive from Hopkins to Maryville but with the threat of IEDs and ambushes. I think it worries me more that the convoy that we're going with came here this morning. This means the route has been traveled already, and they may be expecting a return. I am new to the world of convoying, but that puts some worry on me. I guess I'll find out. After this, I will take a break from leaving. I just want to leave to go home at this point. I'm a little sick of being here. Just so you know, I love all of you, and thank you for everything you've done for me. Deployments are the only way I know to repay all of you.

Part 2

I thought of you tonight, Brittany. My mom said an angel would be on my shoulder, and I believe that was you. I've thought a lot about you tonight; honestly, tonight I've missed you the most I've ever missed you. That convoy here nearly drained me of everything. I cannot wait until these wars are over, and I can come home to you. I was watching TV tonight and a part came on when the wife ran up to her husband and hugged him close and put her arms around him the way to do to me. I wanted to hold you so bad at that moment. I felt you in my arms and very warmly in my heart. You're the best thing that's ever happened to me, and I am thankful every day for you. If distance makes the heart grow fonder, then the gap between us will be filled with the strength of a hundred lifetimes and filled with the warmth of a hundred suns. I love you.

Part 3

How am I going to explain to everyone back home about days like today? Where I was scared to death before the day even started. We shared a building with about 30 local nationals last night. Bosch, another weapons maintenance guy, and I shared a room, and in the middle of the night a guy opened the door and looked in on us. The light woke me, and I looked to see who it was and it was one of the local nationals. He was just staring at us. I looked over at Bosch as he pulled his K bar from his bullet proof vest and tucked it under his sleeping bag. The guy in the doorway closed the door, and nothing happened. We still have no idea what that was all about.

I find myself reflecting later on days like today and why I do this, and I still don't know.

I do know it's going to hurt me when I leave this life. It gives you a sense of purpose because these aren't days of going to work and going home every day. I'm not going to a factory and working my fingers to the bone. These are days of survival, sleeping in rooms with sandbags for windows, and flying through Afghanistan hoping for no issues while on a mission. Why? Because we asked for it, and now we are able to live our lives slower and with more meaning. Ever wonder why when you call home things seem hectic and rarely make sense? It's because when you're away from all of that, home doesn't need to make sense because it's just a place where you think you need to go. The bottom drops out when you reach it. If you are given a reason to live, then you find a way to make it. You got on the wrong plane and left home, and this is home now. I don't know what my mom or Brittany go through on a daily basis, but I understand that I have to comprehend what happens here before I can understand what happens there.

13 Sept. 12

BLACKOUT… Yep, somebody's dead. I've hit that point, and I feel horrible saying it, but it's the truth, and there's no way around it. Any communication with the outside world is put on hold until the next of kin is notified. We're in Sar Hawza, and it's a breeding ground for the Taliban. Their families live here, and they come to visit at night because they know our guys can't pull missions at night. So, the terrorists come and go as they please, and our hands are tied. That is what is happening here. Now I understand the frustration amongst the soldiers who live here. In the next room is a bunch of local nationals. I sleep with my weapon in my sleeping bag, and a knife under my pillow. I don't know how I got here or why I've grown so paranoid, but it's all definitely real and right in my face.

I think of all those people back in Hopkins drinking coffee at Rick's gas station, sitting at Maurice's talking shit on the local gossip. I dunno, it all seems so far away, and I'm here in Afghanistan with nothing but a sandbag between the door and me and some local nationals. The room has windows to our sleeping quarters stacked to the brim with sandbags. This building was most likely someone's house before the war. When we came in and took it over, we turned it into a fort. The sandbags protect anyone living inside from mortar attacks and flying shrapnel and small arms fire. I miss Brittany terribly, and I know she's got to be worried sick about me now. I can't get ahold of her though, not while we're on blackout. I love her so much. She's my rock, and I miss her more and more each day.

> *In the darkness of the night*
> *The strength inside of me shines through*
> *For I am not invincible, but I am awake*
> *I am very aware of what is going on around me*
> *Even before you thought to do it.*

14 Sept. 12

Another morning in Sar Hawza. There is a cat that's outside that sounds like it's dying a horrible death, but I can't seem to find it. That's what I woke up to this morning. I don't know what to say or what to do to help it because I cannot find it no matter how hard I try to locate the sound of its voice. I ran into two guys, one from Savannah and another from Joplin. They're both living here at Sar Hawza. We talked about St. Joe and Maryville and how we definitely missed Missouri. It's nice to find someone from back home. We talked about all of the same places we have been while in the States and how we have probably crossed paths before, but it took us coming to Afghanistan to finally meet.

Brittany told me during our last conversation not to call the guys I work with in the shop fuckface, it was rude. Ha! She was kidding of course. That's how we communicate in the military, not degrading by any means but just the way we talk to one another. I did call Bosch a butthole today, I suppose that is better than fuckface. Regardless, he takes no offense to it. There's some quietness between Chief and me.

Chief and I are in a way kind of like brothers. We get along all of the time, but we do get tired of one another from time to time. That is what living in close quarters with one another for long periods of time will do to you.

I'm not talking as much as I usually do. I guess we're hitting that point in the deployment where we realize we're about halfway through, and your mind goes into autopilot. I listen to this one guy talk, but I know I won't even learn his name because of how lazy and annoying he is. Some people just don't get it. You can't deal with a deployment and people's shitty attitudes. I know that's the way it goes, but I still refrain from having to deal with people like that. I get in a funk, and it's hard to want to be the best version of yourself all of the time. It's the guys who choose to remain that way throughout the whole deployment that really get under my skin. It's not necessary, but it happens.

16 Sept. 12

Last day I believe at Sar Hawza. Things seemed a little tense at work today; everyone was quiet and seemed short tempered. Who knows what that means? Could possibly be that we're all just tired of seeing one another's faces. This place really wears on you after a while. You can tell the difference in bickering and humor between us and the guys who are actually living here. They don't find our humor with one another as funny. I assume that's because they don't see us as one of them, which I understand because they aren't one of us.

We were part of a drill today. We were tasked to man a tower that was only accessed by taking two separate sets of ladders to the top. It reminded me of old fire escape ladders that you would see in movies that took place in big cities. We sat up in that tower for three hours, watching this small village. It was nothing but a drill, and once it was over, we all went back to our room and racked out for the night. I am thankful for these experiences. I think it's great to get away from the metropolis of Sharana for a week and visit these small places. I still feel that my old roommate in Kansas City was right about one thing when he told me, "You hate the people that you are most like." He used to make comments like that all of the time. They wouldn't make sense right away, but over time, I would be confronted with a situation where I finally did understand their meaning. He's a pretty smart guy.

I think I'm realizing that we do get irritated easily with certain people we're most like, and over time, I am working on adjusting my behavior so I can better myself. It's a good thing. I think if one person is really showing a bad attitude then that will affect the rest of us, especially when you're on these small COPs, and you really are cornered most of the time. It becomes a house full of siblings, and no one can get away. There's just so much to enjoy here, like the mountains and scenery, and each other's company. I realize that one day this will be in the past, and I will want to be back. Now is the time to realize this and not in 10 years when I will regret it. I'd rather not take this time for granted. In Iraq, had I not toured Saddam's palace, I would surely regret that by now. I did it though. It took some convincing, but I have that memory, and it's one that will still be with me when I am an old man.

17 Sept. 12

Back to Sharana, and I can't wait to get out of here. There is too much noise and too many people. I really enjoy the seclusion of the smaller COPs. I just don't understand how there can be so much noise in one place. This reminds me so much of when I went home the last time. The things that are going on back home are so chaotic. I think of Sergeant Alexander and how he is most likely having feelings of regret for leaving now. We are all flesh and blood and too much of a good thing can make you sick. Home sometimes is one of these things. Homesick during the deployment can turn into sick of home by the time you get there. That's the beauty of all this in black and white. Modernization has forgotten the romance of war. Our war is a PT fest, the way you should hold a rifle, the way you organize parts. We forget because of these things that people explode while waiting in a chow hall line. That people go off the deep end and shoot each other. Welcome to your waste of time.

22 Sept. 12

The beauty of the world's end...

I spoke with an old friend, Zach, last night. He told me of his recent battle with alcohol. I could easily relate to the words that he shared with me because I, too, have battled with alcohol the past few years. I could feel the cry for help in his writing as we exchanged messages last night, and I know that he could feel from me the helplessness that I conveyed to him. I wrote him of our trying childhoods. Though we had our own separate paths, we both walked very similar ones. We both had our run ins with deadbeat stepdads. His stepdad was very physically abusive while mine was more mentally abusive. We would spend many summers together on the farm at his house in Hopkins listening to Green Day and talking about leaving that town and onto things that were bigger than ourselves. Zach was there when things were at their worst at home, and when things got too tough for one of us, we would jump ship and stay at the other's house until it would blow over. Zach was always a great friend and a good kid. We both were, but I think regardless we experienced enough trauma growing up that it led to us both having troubles as adults. I feel that even though I am in Afghanistan away from alcohol and the distractions of life in the United States, I know they wait for me when I get home. I could easily be right back in his shoes once I get back to the states. At the moment, that is irrelevant, and I wish I could help him, and I hate to see him struggle.

I tried to stay as positive as I could, but it seemed the darkness of each of our stories would not rest. I envisioned a perfect life, a perfect life that neither of us were awarded. In my writing him, I also realized the hard path that I face when I return home. The Army is a slow noose. That tightens when you're back in the States doing regular duties, you deploy, and the noose loosens a bit. Of course, every man struggles in his own way while gone, but we all benefit quite more from the experience of life overseas. When I get home, I wish to face these demons and grasp control of something I've never fully understood. I've never understood why my experiences during my childhood affected so much of my life as an adult. My relationships with others, whether that be with friends or women, have always seemed to be a struggle. I would like one day to fully understand these things.

There is more here than life and the fear of death. The hardest part is the realization and the understanding that you're always in control as long as you accept what you have to do. Most people live life unaware that they are out of control. They never really understand why they do things, they just do them because it's what they've always known. Then suddenly their lives come to a halt because of some big life event like a death or accident, and they are reminded of all the things they take for granted. That's when suddenly their lives open up, and they care more about moments in their lives rather than life in the full spectrum of just living and dying. I appreciate the chance to travel as much as I do and see the things I see because it broadens who I am and makes the world that much more interesting. I care about the people I love and make sure they know what I feel because they could be suddenly gone one day. I one day, too, will have to part ways with this world, and I would rather do that knowing I didn't keep anything I was feeling or thinking to myself.

23 Sept. 12

Super FOB was an endless and vacant place. It still had the best facilities I had encountered yet since I started going on missions supporting the smaller units around Afghanistan and servicing their weapons. I used to have a problem with up and leaving what I was comfortable with, but now, it's second nature, and I enjoy it. I will tell you what I miss though is the comfort of the chairs in Brittany's parents' house and the warmth of her close to me in bed at night. I feel comfortable here to an extent, but I miss her greatly. I just hope that I never take a day with her for granted after this. The land is much flatter here than really anywhere I have ever been. Chief Drakes was telling us about an accident at COP Tillman today. A howitzer crew had gotten the wrong grid coordinates and shot a 155 mm round about 100 yards from the soldiers on an OP. One soldier caught it on his helmet cam, all while he was blown off his feet onto his ass. That's a lot of force for one body to attempt to withstand. The closest we have been is a rocket that hit Sharana last month. It's nothing like Iraq where we were getting mortared every other day.

Our main challenge is ignoring our time left here. It doesn't drag on until you think about the hours or minutes of the day, then it grabs you by the balls and renders you helpless. In the past four years, my time in America and overseas has been pretty evenly dispersed. It's made me appreciate, and let go of a lot of things at the same time. The isolation you experience while on deployment puts you in an isolated mindset, even when you're home. It is very difficult to train yourself to get away from those feelings of isolation once you're back. I think that is what my family complained most about after I returned from Iraq. I wanted to be alone a lot while I would visit them, and I feel it stemmed from being alone so much while on deployment. Flying still puts me on edge every time we leave, and when we're up in the air, I just pray for that feeling of control again that I feel on the ground. I guess once we hit the six month point right around the corner, I'll see light at the end of the tunnel, but I guess until then, I'll just drive on and picture myself somewhere far away from here.

24 Sept. 12

Another day at Super FOB. I can't help but feel like the military is very similar to prison. I suppose you could say prison sentences are much longer than deployments, it's really whatever because they're both the same in their own ways. I'm growing more tired of being here. I find myself having to keep my mind in check. I guess I'm feeling the meaningless sense of being here. I was very angry last night, thinking of home. I can tell when I am away on missions that I feel the distance, then when I get back, I feel anger because of the dumb shit we have to deal with back at Sharana. To me, the Army is there at Sharana, and that means dealing with all of the rules that come with the Army. There is no free thinking or free doing; everything has a rule, and it has to be followed. I really don't like the Army because of that. I daydream a lot about going home. I think it's worse this time because I know what it's like to go home. I want that now. Since I've been gone four months, I'm just tired of leaving, especially now since I have Brittany at home to think about. She just makes me want to be back home that much more, and it makes my time here more difficult.

I'm no longer waiting to get back home and see my friends like on my last deployment. Since I joined the Army, we have all changed quite a bit, and I don't feel as though I am the same around them as I used to be. If I were here and Brittany wasn't waiting for me at home, I feel that my time here would be irrelevant, and it wouldn't feel so much like the minutes and hours were creeping along. I am happy though that I have had the opportunity to be a part of both the wars in Iraq and Afghanistan, but now things are becoming more complex, and I feel as though I have more responsibilities that require me to be home. I know the time will pass and that one day this will all be over, and I will return home, but right now I am stuck in this moment.

1 Oct. 12

From Cloud 9 to six feet under…

My three-year anniversary from the day in Iraq that I will always remember. The day I almost died is what I will remember, or at least felt as though I almost died. I think war gets confusing. Things happen like mortars, and it makes everything confusing. The day I lived and another man died. My first experience with death aside from an elderly grandparent who passed away many years ago. I remember the first mortar attack that we got. I was in my bunk in Iraq and heard the thud of the round hitting the sand, and the phalanx gun going off, and it was so fucking confusing. My roommate at the time was on his second or third deployment, and he just kind of laughed while I ran around like a chicken with its head cut off. It was similar to someone experiencing a tornado siren for the first time. To us from Missouri, a tornado siren isn't really a warning to take shelter. It's when you see shit go flying through your yard and hear the sound as if a train is passing by that's the real warning to take shelter. To someone who hasn't experienced a tornado, you can't get to the basement fast enough once you hear the siren. At the time, I was looking for shelter, and that first mortar attack was my first tornado.

That name resonates with me, Paul Anderson from Dowagiac, Michigan. He was the guy killed on 1 Oct. 09 in Iraq. I read in one of the papers about him and his life. Paul once wanted to deliver a lawn-mower to a family member. The problem was that the family member lived several miles away. So, Paul did it anyway, and when the police would drive by, he would pull into someone's driveway and act like he was just a regular person in the neighborhood mowing their lawn. He would never drive another lawn mower again. He was a month away from finishing that deployment to Iraq. Instead on that night of October 1, 2009 he was skyping his wife when the phalanx system went off and the screams of "INCOMING! INCOMING! INCOMING!" came across the loud speakers. Then a mortar round came through the roof of his room and ended his life.

I have been struggling with depression lately, and there's nothing I can do about it. I could walk into sick call and say I'm feeling down in the dumps and homesick, but every single person in this place is feeling the same way I am. There is no answer to this illness except to lift my head up and drive on. I just don't know how much more drive I have.

12 Nov. 12

Today we formed to see off another soldier wrapped in an American flag. There isn't a lot to say. This time, you could see the body bag exposed under the flag. It felt strange to think that this morning, this guy must have felt the same way that I feel. That we're going home soon, and nothing can stop that. Something did though. I thought of the emotions going through my head. That I have pain in my legs but no regret for running last night. How calm and cool the situation must seem. That the last guy standing in full battle rattle must be his buddy. That this is your second experience with a dead body, and you will think of this quite often once you get home. It is our duty to do as we are told and to die doing what we are told, and we're fine as long as we do what we are told. In all honesty this is a fucking tragedy, and it's happening way too often. There isn't anything cool and calm about it, but this is life now, and we have to treat it as though it's second nature.

Cottrill hit the wall tonight while I had headphones in, and my heart stopped because I thought it was a mortar. My heart said what the fuck for a minute until I realized it was just him swinging his M249 around. War writes its own stories inside you, and you do your best to pretend you have a handle on it. Nothing will compare to this time here. How one man experiences war and how he handles it is his own business. Some handle it well and go on the rest of their lives unscathed by the experiences they encounter. I feel as though it won't be that way for me. I will always remember days like today.

I don't know if I will be able to write for a while. I feel as though the things I am experiencing here in themselves are enough; when I write about them, I am having to relive them again, and these days are taking their toll on me. Do I know any of these guys who have died since we've been here? No. I do know that regardless, the deaths and monotony of life here is taking a toll on me in some way. My mom used to say, "Nick, you have a good heart, and you've always cared so much more than you actually showed." I think she is right. I do care a lot and emotionally in some way just seeing these bodies getting carried through our ranks covered in American flags on their way back to the United States has broken something inside of me. A lot of American mothers lose their little boys in more ways than one.

Every dead body that has been carried through here has a name, and I don't even know any of those names. They grew up in some town in the States, just like I did. They might just be more like me than I know. They might've had a grandpa who taught them how to throw a baseball when they were little like I did. Their mother spent nine months carrying them inside her body, and loved them, and changed their diapers, and took care of them for 18 years, and then sent them out into the world. Now we are sending them back to her in a body bag covered in an American flag. I wish I had the answers to why this has to happen. I often daydream about these guys who have died. I wonder if I had been there could I have helped in some way to keep them alive. I don't care if I know them or not, if they were a good or bad person but I would definitely do what I could to make sure they were able to return home once it's time to go.

13 Dec. 12

I'm glad that grocery stores can send me their crap to throw away. Quite literally I find this stuff in the mail and automatically put it in the trash. Most of it is useless, and I'm not sure who is preparing these lists of items to send us. Similar to most conversation I have, I find no desire in hearing them because most conversations here at this point are feeling meaningless. There is nothing interesting about hearing someone else's day to day life here, as I lead my own and they're exactly the same. So, since getting to Afghanistan, what has changed? Well, I think life got more complex. By complex, I mean just more busy work and less interesting work. We are just putting in our time at this point. I might as well be in a factory back home at this point cranking out batteries or motorcycle parts.

There is no one else that you appreciate more than those who you share your struggles. There is so much more meaning in struggling with someone else, and eventually finding the light in that struggle together. I have no desire to be the best there is at anything.

I just want to pul something out of what I am doing right now in this moment. If that means going against everything that may seem right in order to pull some kind of substance out of life right now then I will do it. It may seem unorthodox to some people, but it's what I take pleasure in. I just want to feel something right now because I am caught up in the monotony of this place, and its fucking wearing me out.

Unfortunately, we are all troubled by just about anything we allow ourselves to be troubled by. Trouble seems to grow at the same rate that good things grow. The consistency in which things flourish in our personal gardens is only as consistent as the hands that place them there. As long as we plant those things, they grow, and produce, but eventually everything will fucking die, regardless of how well you take care of it.

I look at myself in the mirror, and I am not exactly sure how to perceive this man who I am looking at. I am afraid that I no longer have anything in common with the man that I look at in the mirror every day. My assumptions are rarely wrong when it comes to interpretations of myself. I am typically very self-aware and in tune with what I am feeling. I know exactly how I will react at any given moment. The only fear that I have is that I will eventually lose sight of who I am, and that truly a part of me is now broken after our time here. I am not the same man who arrived in Afghanistan all those months ago. I am changed. I worry about how I will acclimate to life back in the states. When it's time to go home, and I load up on that plane and make the trek back to the United States, just what state of mind am I going to be in? This is what concerns me. It's not cut and dry. I don't feel I can sweep this under the rug and just pretend everything is okay, because at times it isn't.

19 Dec. 12

Back on tower guard duties. As our time here starts to dwindle down, that is my place of duty. We are starting to train guys from the Jordanian army on tower guard duties. They will replace us when we leave and head home. I think at first it was a little difficult getting past the language barrier. I have picked up on some Arabic, but just enough to say hello and basic commands for what I need them to do. Grunting and pointing seems to work as well.

The Jordanians are very gentle and kind people. They report to the tower and right away crack open a pot of tea, which they share amongst all of us. I believe it's just a green tea, but I haven't been able to verify that. We watch the valley together and share photos of our loved ones back home, and stories of what life is like in our separate countries. I have befriended one of them whose name is Abu. He seems to be able to understand English better than the others. He's a great guy and has a girlfriend back home in Amman who he plans to marry when he returns. He has taught me some of their written words. It looks like chicken scratches and makes no sense to me, but it passes the time.

Most of the guys that I meet from Jordan are very happy to be here and to be assisting in the war efforts. I have never been to Jordan or even thought about it until this point in my life. I know now though I wouldn't mind one day visiting and seeing what life is like for these boys back home. We might as well have lived on separate planets to this point in our lives, but a war brought us together now, and it may bring us together later down the road if one of us decides to visit the other.

As far as Afghanistan and pulling tower guard duty, explaining that is as simple as the carving that is on the wall in this tower, "It is what it is." We are just putting in our time now until we go home. The war for us is slowing down, and now we wait. I am in better spirits these days, and I think the guys from Jordan are to thank for that. They make me feel like a better person, and I look forward every day to hearing their stories. It makes the passing time easier to manage.

After Everything

10 Feb. 2013

We have an idea of when we will head home, but the dates seemed to change every day. I'm not sure if it is a logistics issue that keeps us here longer or what. Whatever it is needs to be Resolved, so we can get the hell out of here. I am so ready to go home. The last month of this deployment has seemed to drag on. The new unit that was relieving us started moving into our shop, and we really didn't have much to do the last month. The officer who took over for Chief was a real dick, and no one wanted to be around him anyway, not even his own guys. So, I spent a good chunk of my days reading alone in my room and hitting the gym.

I am pretty proud of Cottrill; he hit the gym almost every day that I did this past nine months. He is a taller, skinnier guy, and it's difficult for him to put on weight. So, he ate like a hog and hit the gym at least once a day, sometimes twice. The last night that Leibengood, Cottrill, and I were all in the same room together, I had just turned out the lights, and we all had said goodnight to one another. I had closed my computer screen and lay there in silence. Cottrill always falls asleep the fastest, and you can tell because he breathes heavier than the rest of us when he's sleeping...and when he's awake. Our rooms were divided with plywood walls into four different small sections. The plywood didn't go to the ceiling so you could hear everything that anyone else did.

Leibengood had wanted a little more privacy, so he found some Styrofoam paneling and rigged up a ceiling for his room. That night as I was falling asleep it sounded as though someone was wrestling with a paper sack. I didn't know what it was and actually was so tired, I didn't care. I had just closed my eyes when I heard Cottrill scream, "WHAT THE FUCK!"

I kicked open my door and asked him what was going on.

He said, "Leibengood just crawled over the wall in his underwear and stood by my bed, and said 'Nighty Night.' When I woke up all, I saw was his tighty-whitey ass go crawling through the hole in the ceiling. I just whipped it with my belt."

That last night together was pretty comical. We had plenty of evenings like that though. Even when we were sick to death of each other, we always found a way to get along. We had our good times, but I am ready to put them behind me and finally go home.

12 Feb. 2013

Finally! We clear out our rooms at Sharana and move to tent city. These are the tents where we will be staying while we wait for our flights to go home. The tents are a little further from where we live and closer to where we will fly out of. We are at least making progress to get home, but time is just really creeping along. Staying in this tent is getting old, especially when most of the guys that I have spent the last nine months with have already left on earlier chalks back to the states. I just want to be home. This waiting is starting to piss me off.

I spend a lot of time reading and walking back and forth between tent city and the gym. We are all cooped up in this 12-man tent, and we are sick of each other and the lack of privacy. We've been here a week already. I've heard that we may leave tomorrow, though. Even if we do leave tomorrow, we still will have to spend time in Manas,

Kyrgyzstan, before we get back to the States. It will probably be at least another week and half before we are home.

18 Feb. 2013

We finally arrive at Manas. The great thing about Air Force bases is that you get treated like royalty. I hadn't had ice cream in almost nine months and finally was able to get some. I filled a giant bowl full of as much vanilla ice cream as I could and loaded it with M&Ms and cherries. I didn't care what was on it, I just wanted it. Sitting in the latrine an hour later; I thought I might have overdone it because it was going right through me. It was still worth it though.

We live once again in the tents that we had stayed in when we travelled to Afghanistan.

Nothing has changed. The scenery is still beautiful, but it doesn't call to me anymore. I feel different this time. The first time I was here, I was full of anticipation and excited to be on this adventure. This time, I just want to go home. I don't care as much about it as I did the first time I saw it. I just want to go home. After four days here, we finally get a commercial flight out of Kyrgyzstan and head to Dublin, Ireland. This is the second time I've flown through Dublin; on our way home for leave from Iraq, I went through Dublin Airport. I remembered the currency exchange machines that would exchange American dollars to Euros. I put in one dollar just to get some coins from Ireland and keep around to show my family when I got back home. Most people are buying booze, and I think about getting a bottle of Bushmills Irish Whiskey for my buddy, Ben. He loves that stuff, and I know that he would find it pretty cool to get a real bottle straight from Ireland. Unfortunately, the lines are so long at the register that by the time I get halfway through the check out, it's time to load the plane and make our way back to Topeka, Kansas.

The flights are long – five hours from Kyrgyzstan to Dublin, and then another nine or 10 from Dublin to Topeka. Everyone I'm with is chugging Nyquil in hopes of just sleeping the whole 10 hours. I don't because I don't want to feel groggy once I get home to Kansas. Instead of trying to sleep, I read Clive Cussler's *Raise the Titanic*, one of his books featuring Dirk Pitt. Every time I read that name in the book, I think of Brad Pitt, and I imagine that Brad Pitt is attempting to lift the Titanic from the bottom of the ocean. I am glad it is here to help me pass the time. The book keeps me pretty interested, and I finish it before we land in Topeka.

I spend the rest of the flight remembering the time I came home from Iraq on leave. Tarpley and I travelled together, and about midway through the flight, she fell asleep on my arm.

We were both worn out from being in Iraq for three months. It was nice to have someone I knew to travel with. I left to go back to Iraq the day after Thanksgiving. My family loaded up the car at five in the morning to take me back to Kansas City to the airport. I am from a small town of 500 people, and everyone knows everyone. Mom had stopped at the post office to get her mail before we took off for the airport. I sat in the car staring out the window trying to decide if I was ready to go back or not. In some ways, I was, but in others, I wasn't. Activity at the church across the street caught my attention. Several people were standing around a parked car – a curious sight at 5:00 A.M. As I looked more closely, I realized that it was a county sheriff, and he was covering the body of a kid who had committed suicide a few hours earlier. I had made it through three months of Iraq only to come home and see a dead body here. Leaving on that note felt like a bad omen.

22 Feb. 2013

I am home. I am exhausted, but when you get home from a deployment, you don't just hop right off the bus into the waiting arms of your family. The "Powers that Be" put you in a room for about two hours where you wait until the team back home is ready to officially welcome you with a ceremony. More fucking waiting. At last, we line up in formation and march into a big room where all of our family members are sitting in bleachers. Toby Keith's "Courtesy of the Red, White, and Blue" plays over the speakers (and just for the record, everyone in the military is sick to death of that song and any song by Five Finger Death Punch. They're overplayed, and we need new material). I know Brittany is here somewhere amongst all of these faces, but I have to wait a little longer before I can see her. The ceremony finally comes to a close. When the announcer dismisses us, I stand here waiting for her to come to me. I figure that is the easiest and quickest way for us to get to each other rather than wandering around in this sea of people.

Brittany passes in front of me but doesn't see me. I had waited nine months for this moment, and here she finally was. I froze for a second; I wanted this moment to be special because as soon as we see one another all of the excitement and waiting and anticipation would be over in an instant. After a few seconds of watching her search, I grab her arm and say, "Hey."

She screams, "Oh, my God!" at the top of her lungs, and I pick her up in my arms and kiss her like I have never kissed her before.

Nine months have passed, and this is the best welcome home gift I could have ever dreamed of. My grandparents, my mom, my sister, and Brittany's parents are all here. I had asked Chief Sprague, who had left Afghanistan a month before me, to meet me at the redeployment center at Fort Riley. He promised to be there with a six pack. I couldn't wait to see him and have a beer with him. As promised, Chief meets me out in the parking lot to say hi and welcome back. I am glad to see him, but I think he has his own stuff to do, and right now, beer is the last thing I want. I just want to get the three-hour drive back to Maryville over.

You forget about certain things when you're on a deployment. You don't drive for nine months and being in a car once again is weird at first. You stop at a restaurant, and seeing everyone so relaxed and living without a care in the world even seems odd. Like I've said before, you go from one minute living in a country that's at war, and the next minute you're back to Mayberry, where everyone has been living life untroubled by war ever since you left. I guess I just feel more observant. The actions of other people seem odd to me, they just wander around without thought and very passive without any real hurry in their stride. I think this all has to do with being gone nine months and spending a lot of time reflecting on my own actions. I bet from the perspective of someone else in the restaurant my actions are probably odd as well, like I'm watching everyone like a hawk. All of it feels foreign, even though it is home. I am excited to see everyone, but the atmosphere is so loud and overwhelming. Everyone wants to hug me. I only want to hug Brittany. I just want some peace and quiet and to appreciate not being on a plane anymore.

The homecoming isn't anything special, and I had requested that. I don't want to end up in the ER like I did when I came home from Iraq. This time, I want things to be a little easier, and I just want to spend time with Brittany. She is exhausted from the long day, though, and goes to bed early. Since my body hasn't adjusted to the time difference yet, I stay up to keep from disturbing her rest. I spend the evening drinking beer at her parents' house and just bullshitting with her brother. Everything feels right. I am happy and content to finally be home, so Brittany and I can move on with our lives together. Tomorrow night, we are going to my good friend Paul's parents' house for a little welcome home party. I'm looking forward to seeing my friends. Paul and his dad, Mick, had brewed a porter beer to celebrate my return. They called it "The Rucker Porter." Porters during winter seemed to always be my favorite, and I looked forward to the opportunity to put on some extra pounds guilt free, and a real stout porter was sure to do that.

I wake up around the same time Brittany's parents do. They show me the ring that we had been collaborating on the past few months. It was a lot bigger in person than what I remembered seeing in the photos. I slip it in my pocket and wait for her to wake up. I had on sweatpants, and this giant bulge in my pocket from the ring box was a dead give away that I was probably up to something. I sit on the bed later that morning as she was getting ready for us to head to St. Joe for the day. I just sat there watching her do her hair. She asked me what I had done last night after she went to bed. I told her that I just stayed up watching a movie and talked to her brother until around two in the morning. The small talk wasn't really helping the that fact that I was so nervous and wasn't sure exactly how I was going to approach her with popping the question. After sitting there quiet and giving very short answers to all her questions for about 30 minutes, I could tell she was starting to suspect something. I felt as though it was time, I finally take the ring out of my pocket and put it on the dresser next to her. She says, "What is this?"

"Open it and check it out," I say. She opens it and is silent for a second and then screams. I take the case and get down on one knee, using the very little room we had between the bed and dresser. "Will you marry me?" I ask.

She, of course, says yes. She couldn't contain her excitement and ran into the kitchen to share the good news with her parents. They, of course, have been aware of this plan for quite some time, so they entertain her excitement. The whole day she held me close. It was as though just us being engaged brought us even closer. We spent the day in St. Joe shopping for clothes because everything I had before I left for Afghanistan was either old or didn't fit. We had to be back to Maryville earlier though because we planned to go to my welcome home party that evening in Bedford, Iowa, with my friends the Wares. It was about a 30-minute drive, and we were planning to stay at my dad's.

We made our way up to Bedford once we got home. Mick and I had planned this party while I was still in Afghanistan, and it is to be my official homecoming party. Mick shares stories of traveling through Iran in the Peace Corps when he was in his twenties. Mick can tell one hell of a story and has a way of keeping you wanting more. Some people in our lives teach us patience and appreciation for life and its beauties and wonders. Mick and his son Paul do that for me. Paul has always been one of the most knowledgeable people that I know and over the years has introduced me to some of the best movies I have ever seen. We share stories of my time in Afghanistan, talking and laughing, and drinking until the wee hours of the morning. There is no cell phone reception or distractions. This is exactly where I want to be tonight – with good people whom I care about.

As the months after the deployment passed, I started to struggle with alcohol. I loved Brittany and wanted to be the best man that I could for her, but I always put alcohol ahead of her. Red flags started to surface. I wasn't drinking to have a good time, I was drinking until I blacked out, and then she would have to babysit me for the evening. She was starting to notice a pattern, I knew that she was because I was starting to feel a pattern as well. She wasn't liking what she saw, and I didn't know how to fix it. I had started to feel the pressure from her, I would order a beer at a restaurant, and I would get a look from her that basically said, "Is that really a good idea?" I think it only made it worse rather than initiated any positive change in me.

Many times, we discussed whether getting married was a good idea. I was still living at Fort Riley, and she was finishing school in Nevada. We saw each other once a month. During the weeks I started drinking more and more heavily. I knew what I needed to do in order to prepare for marriage, but it just wasn't happening. I had a mental block in my brain that I would feel when the stress level of marriage talk would grow intense. Instead of proactively trying to better the situation, I'd find refuge in alcohol. I was starting to hide the addiction that was growing, and at the time that's all I could do.

We had discussed the finances for the wedding and who was going to pay for what. I paid for the photographer. Her parents paid for everything else. I had to break into my Afghanistan savings for that because I couldn't save a dime anymore. All of my money was going to beer after work. I would just lie and say I was saving, but really all I had planned to do was pull money out of savings to pay for the photographer. That was the money that I had saved from Afghanistan, and what I had left after buying the ring.

I didn't know how bad things were until her bridal shower. I showed up when it was about over. We went down into the basement of her parents' house, and she cried in my arms and said she didn't know if this was the right decision. I feel like Brittany had always been very grounded and sure about everything she was doing throughout her life. I suddenly was becoming something she wasn't so sure of, and it was starting to show through these actions. Hearing these words broke my heart, but it wasn't enough to change the fact that I was becoming an alcoholic. I smiled and assured her that things were going to get better and that we just needed to give it time. Did I really care? No, I didn't really feel anything, and her reactions were starting to show that she knew that I didn't. I didn't know how to tell her what was going on.

I just assumed that the alcohol would eventually work itself out. I had heard stories from family members about struggling with alcohol and how one day they just woke up and quit drinking cold turkey. I placed all my chips on the hope that it would work that way for me too. I faked the honesty quite well and covered up one lie with another lie. Slowly the noose around my neck started to tighten. I was in denial, and my denial was only buying me time. I knew in my heart that eventually I would have to face this. I believe the fear of letting her down or possibly losing her is what kept me going at the time. She wasn't happy. Neither was I, but I promised that we would work this out and everything would be fine.

Your love's an anchor
I'm in your sea
Swaying back and forth
Trying to stay on my feet
No rhyme or reason
It's come down to this
Know that I
Hope you feel, everything
After you read this.

Brittany and I were married on September 21, 2013. I had gotten home from Afghanistan on the 22nd of February 2013 and proposed to her the next morning. I felt as though it was rushed, as though the decision wasn't fully thought through. I have always been the type to jump in head first into a situation without really weighing all of the pros and cons. In the moment, it felt like a great idea. With all of the excitement coming home from Afghanistan, this would be the icing on the cake and a happy ending to a nine-month long war story. We had rushed the engagement, and now we felt like we were at a point of no turning back with the wedding. So much of her parents' money had gone into it, and I think she felt trapped. I just wanted to keep going on because I really didn't want to lose her. No matter how much you want to keep someone in your life, if you're not willing to face the issues you have head on, then the relationship will fail. That is what was slowly happening.

Two weeks before the wedding, I was drunk in the barracks at Fort Riley. It was a Thursday, and I started drinking as soon as I got off work at five. I was getting pretty drunk and was trying to do laundry at the same time. I was going downstairs to the laundry room when I tripped on the top step of the staircase and hit my face on the hand rail as I was going down. I was bleeding like a stuck pig and made my way down to the CQ desk in the barracks, and Coffman, a guy in my unit, was on duty.

When he saw my face, he immediately said, "Oh, shit!"

I barely remember any of it. He took me to the ER on post, and my NCO at the time, Sergeant Lamberti, came to help me out. I avoided calling Brittany because I knew she would know that I was drinking if she heard me talk, and that it would just break her heart. They sewed my face up and gave me the next day off.

I looked like hell, and finally called her the next day to let her know what had happened.

She was concerned, but I didn't give her too many details. Still, she had to have known I was drinking when it happened. I ended up going back to her parents' that night. Here we were, two weeks from the wedding, and I looked like Freddie Krueger with my face all messed up. That was when she really started to question our upcoming wedding. She didn't say anything to me, but I knew just by her demeanor that she wasn't happy. The tensions were high leading up to the day of the wedding.

She had spent most of our wedding day worrying that I would get drunk before we even got to the actual ceremony. My longtime friend, Ben, was a groomsman and was there by my side during most of the ceremony. We both had a long history of drinking together, and it had never really posed an issue until we got older and started involving women in our lives. At the time of my marriage, he was going through a divorce, and on my wedding day, it was obvious that things were not good, at least he didn't seem like himself. I didn't blame him for feeling uncomfortable, but he wanted to be at my wedding, and that's what mattered the most to me. Ben has always been my best friend through thick and thin, but I felt that there was little I could do for him that day. I wanted to drop everything and help him, but I felt like I couldn't. I had too much going on that day, and I found it hard to help my best friend and get married at the same time. In some strange way, I feel as though maybe by my ignoring what was going on with Ben, somehow my own issues with my relationship would go away.

The night before the wedding, I promised Brittany that I wouldn't get drunk and would show up on our wedding day in tip top shape. That would be a promise that I would break. We spent most of the night running around Maryville, Missouri, and partying with whoever was willing to party with us, spreading the word that tomorrow, I was going to be a married man. My friend Nathan, who would be playing guitar during our wedding, was the only voice of reason that night. He had invited me to go up to the local pub and watch the Kansas City Royals game, and we could just have a chill evening and go to bed early. I had no interest in that at all. I would layer my excuses until eventually I got what I wanted, and that was to stay up until the wee hours of the morning drinking myself into oblivion.

The morning after our wedding, I woke up with very little recollection of what had happened. If Brittany was expecting a fairytale wedding and end to the night, I definitely did not follow through. These events from our wedding night would soon enough come back around, and I would eventually have to face them. I didn't even make it past the living room, I passed out on the floor in front of the TV. We had this conversation numerous times, about how things just had gone downhill from the beginning. I am fully to blame for that. I was definitely not ready for the level of commitment that accompanied marriage. I could barely take care of myself. At the time, I was still in the Army on active duty, and everything during the week was taken care of. I had a place to live, clothes on my back, and food. I rarely had to worry about taking care of myself.

Alcohol had never done a positive thing for me, and I often wondered why I had let it gain so much control over me. At what point did I allow it to become a crutch? I didn't know who I was if I wasn't slightly under the influence. I simply could not exist in this world without altering my perception somehow with liquor. Little did I know that I was not equipped with the necessary skills to overcome alcoholism in time to save our marriage. It was over before it even began. Who was to blame? Me. I could point fingers any direction I wanted to at the time, but all fingers pointing back at me outnumbered the one I pointed in someone else's direction.

March 2014, I was headed to Fort Polk Louisiana to JRTC (Joint Readiness Training Center). Brittany told me before I left that our marriage was coming to an end. I was about to go 21 days without communication with the outside world. I was miserable those 21 days. The only thing that even turned around my bad attitude about the trip was a conversation I had in a laundry room in the barracks at Fort Polk. First Sergeant Burky pulled me aside because he knew something was wrong and that I could use a little direction. We talked about what was going on. I believe at the beginning of that conversation I had every intention of trying to get out of training and go home. He would not allow that, and I thank him every day that he didn't let me go back because it was preparing me for what was to come. He shared his experiences of his time in a similar situation, and it helped me to better understand that life would be okay and to move on. I stuck it out with hopes that she would come around. We finally got our phones back at the end of the 21 days. Sadly, nothing had changed. Her mind was made up. I didn't blame her. I had given her every reason to walk away. Even though she was unhappy, we still held onto hope for a few more months and kept trying to make our marriage work.

I do remember the day that it was set in stone. We had spent the weekend celebrating Cottrill's bachelor party in Junction City, Kansas. I had gotten obliterated drunk, and it was the straw that finally broke the camel's back. I could barely stand on my own. She left and made the three-hour drive back to Maryville that night. I woke up the next morning wondering what had happened. I couldn't remember anything that had happened at all. I couldn't get in touch with her that next morning and honestly had no idea why. I could not recollect the events that had taken place the night before. All I remembered was a few foggy moments of her angry with me and loading up in her car to head back to our apartment before I blacked out.

I didn't know what to do at the time, so I drove back to Maryville to try and fix things. They were beyond fixing at that point. I stayed at my aunt's while trying to work things out. I had to let my aunt know what was going on because it was unlike me to visit Maryville and not stay with Brittany. I made myself out to be the good guy in the situation. It was hard to do at this point because my world was starting to fall apart, and I was starting to fall apart. She was shocked and wanted to help in any way that she could, but words could relieve the frustration and pain I felt.

During the week of July 4th, Brittany picked me up from my aunt's house one morning. We drove out to a park in Maryville. We talked, and Brittany said that she wasn't going to go on with someone who acted like this, and at the time, I promised I would change, but I wasn't capable of that level of change. As we talked, I was hurt and frustrated and wanted to just go back to my aunt's and leave this whole situation behind me. I didn't realize that these few moments would be the last moments that we would have together. We sat parked on the road outside of my aunt's house. She told me she wanted a divorce. This was the first time I had heard her actually say it. I took my ring off my finger and slid it down the straw of a cup that was sitting in the middle console of the car. The weight of that ring sliding down the straw matched the tremendous amount of weight I felt slide down and hit me in the gut. It was the hardest thing I had ever done in my life. I had made it through a deployment and made it a point to make it back to her, and I let all of that slip away. I told her I loved her and that I always would, forever. I got out of the car, slowly walked back up the driveway, and stopped. I turned around in hopes that she would ask me to come back. She didn't; it just never happened. I stood there and looked at her sitting in her car. I didn't know what to do, so I threw in the towel. The love was still there, but the damage had been done.

I walked back into the house and cried more than I think I ever have before. It was over. We were over. That was the last time we saw each other. I cried until I guess I finally ran out of tears, and there was nothing left. The crying was replaced with a dull aching feeling in the my stomach... I had to pull myself together though because I was the best man in Cottrill's wedding that week. It was a miserable week but I asked for every bit of it. An upcoming divorce didn't slow my drinking down. I think if anything, it made it worse, or I made it worse.

We were divorced by October of that year. I would have a mental breakdown in July before the divorce was final. My first bout with suicide. Yes, suicide. I didn't want to live anymore. I could not get a handle of my life no matter what direction I turned, and I was blind to the fact that alcohol was to blame. So, I sent up the white flag and surrendered, a real ballsy move on my part. A real selfish move, but necessary. Take me away, and let's fix my brain, I said. My fucking brain was littered with beer bottles and whatever trash I could cram into it. I spent a week in a mental health facility in Newton, Kansas.

We had classes that were structured around our mental disorders. I spent one hour a day painting pictures that expressed my current feelings or moods. I would then spend an hour passing a ball around the room for exercise. We would talk about why we were patients there. I heard many inspirational stories. During my days there, I heard many inspirational stories. But the nights brought fear and desperation. I could hear other patients screaming and beating on the doors. Some even got out of their rooms. I kept my door locked. We had to lock our doors from the inside at night to make sure that no one got in our rooms when we were asleep. The only comfort I found was from a visit with my family, who made the trip to see me. I promised them I was going to stop drinking and that it was time to move on with my life. *Bullshit*, I thought. I was just waiting until the moment they turned me loose, and I would be right back at the liquor store ready to slam beers once again.

That is what I did. I got released after nine days and didn't drink for the first two. I was assigned a counselor through the Army, but after two days, I was back at it. She would ask me how my sobriety was going, and I would lie. I would say, "It's going great and the medication is working now for depression." I, of course, wasn't taking the medication. I didn't need it. I had alcohol to keep me company.

When did alcohol become a problem for me? I had been drinking off and on since I was 21. For most of my life, I have felt lost. Alcohol was my way of relieving stress. Sometimes I would take a break from drinking, but it never lasted longer than a week. I would start to feel better both mentally and physically, then as soon as I convinced myself I could manage my drinking better and do this casually, I was right back down the rabbit hole.

Last night, I had a dream, a dream like none I had never before. In the dream, I woke in my bed. I could hear a grumbling coming from the closet across the room. It sounded like deep breathing, puffing in and out, in and out. I stood up and slowly walked over towards the closet door. I wasn't scared or startled but at ease. I walked slowly as I heard the deep breaths push in and out against the inside of the door. I suddenly envisioned while in the dream a bear in

the woods. Breathing heavily in the woods, just cool enough to show traces of its breath as it came from its mouth. In that moment, I knew what was behind that door. I flashed back to my closet door. I put my ear against it and heard its breath going in and out in and out. Then the bear grew quiet, and he echoed the words, "Wake up."

I awoke from that sleep and had no idea what I had experienced. To this day, I am piecing that dream together.

23 Apr. 16

In and out of consciousness… "What the fuck happened, and why is my grandpa in the room?"

Oh yeah, a few hours ago I tried to commit suicide or threatened it, and now here I am in the hospital with a blood alcohol content of .3 something and no fucking clue what happened from about 6 A.M. to 12 P.M. this afternoon. I do remember going to see Jeff Dunham last night, and chugging tall boys during the show. Going back to Erik's house and continuing to drink well into the night. I woke up around 6 A. M. and drove home.

I didn't want the party to end. I polished off the six pack that was in my refrigerator. I drank IPA's so the ABV on that particular beer per bottle was around 12 percent. Take into consideration that I was already still drunk from the night before. This was just me compiling more and more on top of the shit storm that was already in full swing.

I ran out of beer around 10 A.M., and suddenly, I was in panic mode. I was still responsive and hadn't passed out yet. So why not get an Uber and head to the gas station? I've been down this road before, and on Sundays, you can't buy beer until 11, so I had to kill a little time. I was in a dark and very bad place. I was in between crying and was slowly walking to the ledge of my mind, waiting to jump. I just needed enough alcohol to make that happen.

11:00 A.M. rolls around, and I make it to the gas station. Two more six packs of O'Dell IPA ought to do it. Sure enough, it did. I got no more than four into that first six pack, and the lights went out. I was on autopilot. I was a fucking mess, but it wasn't anything that I hadn't experienced before. I would drink until I would black out, and the only way I could piece together what happened the night before was to look at my call list or text messages. I don't remember what pushed me over the edge. I honestly believe that I was just tired. I wasn't making any progress with life. I wasn't fully applying myself to my music, and it showed on stage. The alcohol was putting the nail to the coffin. I picked up that gun and even in and out of consciousness, I remember putting it in my mouth and tears running down my face onto the barrel. I hit a moment during this where I knew that this wasn't how it needed to be. I remember leaning my head against the barrel and letting the gun hold my weight up. I finally picked up my phone and was crying and called Erik and said, "Man, you need to come get me because I've got a gun in my mouth, and I'm not okay. I don't want to die man, but I can't keep living like this." It was a very troubling yet eye opening time. I don't know if I was more confused than Erik and Rachelle, but I knew that something had to be done, and I couldn't be in control of starting it.

Erik has always been there for me. Through the deployments and through life since both of them. I think that if you look up the definition to a friend in the dictionary, you will find his face. I owe a lot to him and the things that he has done for me. This was going to be the ultimate test of our friendship. I called on him because, regardless of the situation, I knew that he would show up. He has always known the right thing to do in any given situation that I've been in with ,him, and I trusted him that day with my life. I am thankful every single day for him.

Erik and Rachelle showed up and I barely remember what happened after that. I know I could barely walk and they had to help me get from my apartment to my car. They took me to the Omaha VA, where they confirmed that I was lucky to still be alive given the amount of alcohol I had in my system. It was no surprise to me; it was just another day not a Saturday. See, I had been doing this to myself day in and day out going on a year now. I was surprised my body had survived that long and I didn't one night fall asleep and not wake up. Jeff Dunham was just the occasion which had me drinking in public and not alone at home. I had been very comfortable drinking alone with myself; it was my way of hiding the life I was leading.

I was half in and out of consciousness, and I remember that bear, and him saying wake up. Instead it really wasn't a bear this time, it was my grandpa, and he was trying to get my attention. I had a long history of getting hammered and drunk dialing him late at night. I would do this for a while and then eventually when I would call and ask for him, my grandma would ask, "Nick have you been drinking?" It would break my heart to hear her say that. I would remember in those moments when I was a kid, sitting on my grandpa's lap in his recliner watching *Harry and the Hendersons* and laughing and feeling the love. I would then take a break from calling for a while and let the damage blow over. This was no one's fault but my own. If my family or anyone ,affected by my actions during this time ever felt guilty as though they should've done something then I just have to say that it was not your fault or your place to change my life; it was my own and

I have done my best to do that since then. This is now a constant effort to consistently disrupt the old patterns that I had, so that I can secure a future that I enjoy day in and day out. It is a constant struggle, but a struggle that is well worth the reward.

I woke up in that emergency room.

My grandpa said to me in his own way, "Nick, it's time to get yourself together." This was a very important day in my life. Something came over me in that moment that led me to believe that the rest of the days of my life wouldn't be easy, but they would be worth it. He set the groundwork, I just had to do the work. The nurses came in and hooked me up with a banana bag and watched me overnight. I was close to death from alcohol poisoning. The main doctor who was looking over me offered me a 28-day rehab program. I didn't even hesitate and said that I would do it. That was a huge decision, and one that I had a feeling would change my life.

I had a week to get ready for rehab after I was discharged from the hospital. I never once questioned whether this was a good decision or not. I just knew that it was going to change my life. I didn't know exactly how, but I knew that it was going to. If you look at your daily life and what you're putting all of your energy into, you can't lie to yourself. You can lie on social media and to your friends but you cannot lie to yourself. I had to be upfront with me and who I was. I was an alcoholic, and now looking back, it wasn't just a couple of years of alcohol abuse, it was 10 years of running the same habits. Habits are defining, not just to everyone around you but to yourself as well. If I was having an issue with justifying why I would drink on any given evening, all I would have to do is turn on the TV, or open up social media, and I would look for an enabler. A justifiable reason to open a bottle that night. If someone was celebrating a birthday and posted a photo of themselves drinking on social media and having a good time, then that was my reason that night. I was looking for anything.

I showed up to rehab and roomed with this guy who lived in the same town my grandparents live in. This was significant because they live in a town of 192 people. I thought to myself, awesome a silver lining, and life has brought these two people together to get through this time in their lives together. The reality is, we didn't hit it off. We were completely different people, and he had no intentions of getting better. He ended up asking to leave the room we shared; I think he had some more serious mental health issues, and his moods were all over the place. He switched rooms and ended up having issues with the next guy that he roomed with. I did find out later after leaving rehab that his wife died suddenly after we left and that he was in question. I believe they finally chalked it up to suicide.

The people I met in rehab ranged from drug addicts to alcoholics. I friended a couple, and Christian and Jason were the main two that I spent my time with. The great thing is that we all at one point were veterans, so we had some common ground regardless. I spent a lot of time to myself, just with my thoughts. The withdrawal in the beginning was pretty horrible. I couldn't sleep, and my hands shook, and I just would sweat at times for no reason. I had panic attacks at the oddest times, and I knew that if I got through this and survived the trenches of this time with alcohol withdrawal that the outcome would be significant.

One thing I picked up on is that, yes, I did deploy, and life was a struggle at times, but there are many guys who went out and went face to face with war every day. They came home and some had real issues, and some were completely fine, but everyone experienced it in a different way. I realized that we definitely are not all the same and that war affects us all differently. I wasn't sitting there screaming, "Give me disability and money and let me go on my merry way." No, I was simply saying that I've got these fucking issues that are taking a toll on my life, and I need some help. But I wanted to help myself, and I felt like I was taking an opportunity away from someone who was unable to help himself. I felt that I was taking up space for someone who really needed to be in the hospital. In all honesty, it has been a struggle to understand my time in the hospital. My time in the hospital was confusing because I felt as though I didn't need the help and could face this on my own. This, of course, was a lie I would tell myself because I didn't want to blame my problems on anything that was war related. In all honesty it may not have been 100 percent war related, but it did have a little to do with my issues.

I met many guys who were just like me in the VA system. They didn't want a hand out, but they wanted answers and help. For some of us, it was easy to ask for help, and for others, they were dropped off at the front door without really wanting to be there. I, of course, needed a break from the routine of what I was doing, which was drinking an 18-pack of beer a night. You watch those shows like intervention and say to yourself that, "this isn't me," or "that won't ever be me." The sad fact was that it was me, and I was out of control and needed uprooted from my life in order to fix it.

After 28 days, I left. I knew that if I was going to stay ahead of this, then I needed to find something that was going to work for me. I knew that when I was in Iraq, that was the best shape of my life that I had ever been in. Benjamin Bernard Villa would kick my ass every single day, we would lift weights and run and lift random stuff like concrete and climb concrete T walls and I ran my best two-mile time then. I needed to find a way to make that my routine now and get back in shape both mentally and physically. I needed to live my life like I was on a deployment – fewer distractions and a laser-focus on very few things. So, I googled gyms close by, and the first one that popped up was Iron Hero. I walked in to do my baseline workout, which involved 500 m row, 40 air squats, 30 sit ups, 20 pushups, and 10 pull ups. I did this, and for the first time in my life, I threw up after a workout. I knew right then that this was the place that I needed to be. Now two and a half years and 500 classes later, guess what, it happened. I am in the best shape of my life and because I got rid of my TV and now listen to podcasts and read books and play music and network, and I don't party and don't go out at all and only take part in things that I am interested in. I am getting the things that I wanted. I'm not making a killing, but I am happy. That is the hardest thing to accomplish, being happy.

I have spent more time in bars now not drinking than I did when I was drinking. I spend most nights picking through the strings of a guitar playing music. My story is heard through my songs and mainly in the lyrics I write. I often think back to those times in Iraq and Afghanistan and still miss them to this day, but I understand that they're in the past, and as important of a time as they were, it's okay to let them go. I have yet to write any songs about deployments or the military, and I think it's all because so many people have done it in the past. I would prefer not to be known as "the guy who plays patriotic music." I will leave those songs to other artists. I don't feel as though I have anything against patriotic songs or music, but I just feel like I served my time, and I am still serving my time, and I would rather my music and military not intertwine.

Cross-fit and music and laser focus on the things I want have become my AA program. I won't lie; I am still not perfect. I waste a lot of time on social media and worrying about what people think about me, but I am aware of that, and I work on that day to day in order to get better. It takes time to get past the bad habits we create for ourselves. I always remind myself that it took me three years to put on an extra 30 pounds and most likely it will take me three years to take it off as well. This goes the same with all habits that we create in our lives. Do I still think about Brittany? At times, she crosses my mind. I put out an album back in 2015, and a lot of the songs that I put out then were my way of saying goodbye. I needed somewhere to focus my attention, and music was the outlet. I wrote a song called "Love You a Little Longer," and I think that song really emphasized where my head was then. I knew what I had to do to let her go, but I just did not want to. As time passes by, so do the memories I still play "Love You a Little Longer" to this day at just about every show. The feeling never really changes. I just pick up that guitar now, and when I start to play it, it reminds me of how far I've come and how much has changed. Overcoming adversity is not an easy task. At one point, I wanted to die, and now I couldn't even imagine having those thoughts. In emotional weight, I have shed some much-needed pounds over the past few years. I believe the hard times I've faced in my life greatly shaped the man that I am today, and in a way, I'm glad they happened, because it was necessary. I do my best now to try and help others through my experiences.

In high school, I had an issue with one particular guy, and at one point, he tripped me down a flight of stairs, which is why I now have a fake tooth in the front of my mouth. I never was one to lash out in anger, and I assumed even at the time that he probably was an unhappy individual and probably had a troubled home life. I was angry about the situation though, and the only way that I knew how to fix this was to write about it. I wrote for two hours after I got home from the dentist that day. I wrote until my fingers hurt. At the end of writing that, I read back through what I had written and what I had was a letter. A letter to this guy who had knocked me down those stairs. I said it's not your fault, I wasn't asking for it, but still it's not your fault. At the end of the letter, I wrote I that I wanted to share this with him because today I realized that the answer isn't getting angry and pointing the blame at others and continuing this cycle, that it means either helping someone else realize their fault or accepting blame for a fault. I never gave him the letter. I kept it in our house in a Nike shoe box until it was subject to water damage during a house fire we had in 2008.

Sometimes, when I felt like a situation was going to get the best of me, I would pull that letter out and read it. It helped many times, and after writing this and the story that started back in 2008, I realize that I am still very much the man who wrote that letter many years ago – soft at heart and wanting to help others. That is why I joined the Army and why I volunteered for deployments and why I now make music. One factor has baffled me the past few years is why the alcohol? Well, I've come to believe that some events in our lives happen, and we may not fully understand them or aren't able to comprehend exactly just how much of an effect it has on us. I forgot how to help myself, and I lost sense of the man who wrote that letter so many years ago. This book is a reminder to myself to remember that guy, and I hope that you, too, are able to find that person within yourself.

Black Swan Rises

ON APRIL 23, 2015, my whole life changed. As I spoke about earlier, that was the day that I finally got my shit together in an emergency room at the VA in Omaha, Nebraska. Since that time, it has been a struggle at times to keep my life together. I've had many setbacks, but I've also had many victories. I think of it this way. Have you ever had a dream that seemed so real that it was almost as though it were really taking place? You wake up, and a month or a year or five years down the road, you have a sudden moment of deja vu, and it brings back memories from that dream, as though parts of that dream had somehow leaked over into reality. Those moments really can be kind of frightening and exciting at the time, like the universe is sending us a message that something very important is about to take place in our lives, these could come to us in dreams that we have or those moments of déjà vu . The alcoholic side of me found a way to leak itself into the man that I am today, I find myself wanting to take a drink from time to time, or I fall into old habits of negative thinking.

When I was drinking, I did not feel like I was good enough for the world around me. I fixated so much on the negative moments in my life that I wasn't even aware that life holds so many positive moments. I had a place to sleep, a job, and I had music. I was always willing to let those things go in a heartbeat if it meant that I could stay up one more hour to continue drinking on any given night. I spent a lot of time in the past and rarely thought about the future. A lot of work has been done since I parted ways with alcohol to reverse all of that negative thinking. Then I had an idea, what if I had something that could constantly remind me of just how far I had come.

In 2008, a St. Louis based rock band, Story of the Year, put out an album called *The Black Swan*. I loved the album art on the cover of the CD. I decided then that if I ever get a tattoo, I am going to get that black swan tattooed somewhere on my body. I never really had a justifiable reason to get this tattoo though. Regardless, I started formulating my reasoning for this tattoo. I came up with this conclusion. We are born into innocence, and during that time we are white swans and truly bear no significant scars. As we mature, experiences shape who we are. We go through tough times and life really kicks the shit out of some of us. We start to lose that innocence through the consistent suffering that we may put ourselves through and our white feathers overtime start to change colors. Those feathers take on a new black color. As we start to regain control of our lives we never forget about those times when we were white swans, but we learn to appreciate our lives today as black swans and the struggles we went through to earn that color of feathers.

In 2016, I finally had enough reasoning to get that tattoo. I had a year of sobriety under my belt and finally a justifiable reason to get the black swan tattooed on my forearm. Today, the tattoo is a constant reminder to me that at one point, life wasn't so beautiful, but I was able to find a silver lining through sobriety. If I start to question this journey that I am on with sobriety, then I just have to look down at my right forearm, and I'm reminded to keep going. This book I hope find its way into the hands of those who need it, those who are struggling with either alcohol or depression. Life gets tough, and as easy as it is to throw in the towel, you have to push passed the time cap in order to grow I hope you're able to understand that your life does matter, even if sometimes it may seem meaningless. We are all in this together. We are all one team.